CONCERT SOUND
AND LIGHTING SYSTEMS

Third Edition

CONCERT SOUND
AND LIGHTING SYSTEMS

Third Edition

John Vasey

**Focal
Press**

Boston   Oxford   Auckland   Johannesburg   Melbourne   New Delhi

Focal Press™ is an imprint of Butterworth–Heinemann.

Copyright © 1999 by John Vasey

Butterworth–Heinemann

A member of the Reed Elsevier group

Recognizing the importance of preserving what has been written, Butterworth–Heinemann prints its books on acid-free paper whenever possible.

 Butterworth–Heinemann supports the efforts of American Forests and the Global ReLeaf progam in its campaign for the betterment of trees, forests, and our environment.

Library of Congress Cataloging-in-Publication Data

Vasey, John.
    Concert sound and lighting systems / John Vasey. — 3rd ed.
      p.   cm.
    Includes bibliographical references and index.
    ISBN 0-240-80364-7 (alk. paper)
    1. Theaters—Electronic sound control. 2. Stage lighting.
  3. Concert tours. I. Title.
  TK7881.9.V37 1999
  621.389'2—dc21   99-30654
                                           CIP

British Library Cataloguing-in-Publication Data
A catalogue record for this book is available from the British Library.

The publisher offers special discounts on bulk orders of this book.
For information, please contact:
Manager of Special Sales
Butterworth-Heinemann
225 Wildwood Avenue
Woburn, MA 01801-2041
Tel: 781-904-2500
Fax: 781-904-2620

For information on all Focal Press publications available, contact our World Wide Web home page at: http://www.focalpress.com

10 9 8 7 6 5 4 3 2 1

Printed in the United States of America

CONTENTS

PREFACE

Good sound and lighting are the foundation of any concert; poor sound ruins the audience's enjoyment of the concert, and poor lighting destroys the dramatic impact of the performance. Good sound and lighting systems enhance a concert, create interest, and command attention. Production excellence, however, is not easy to achieve.

I wrote this book to establish a foundation for sound and lighting equipment personnel and to offer necessary information on the exceedingly diverse subjects associated with concert production. This book is intended to provide clear, practical guidance for people interested in working with today's sophisticated production technologies. It is not, however, intended in any way to replace or reduce the need for practical training.

For those of you already working in sound and lighting fields, the information in *Concert Sound and Lighting Systems* may serve as a source of reference; equipment operation is explained in detail. Because there are no fixed rules for operating sound or lighting consoles, it is not possible to include the artistic elements of operation beyond the most basic concepts. Once you learn how the equipment works, your imagination is free to realize its full potential.

If you are just beginning your career in sound and lighting, you will soon realize that the more prepared you are for a job, the easier and more enjoyable the job will be. After each show one always asks, "Could I have done better?" The answer always is, "Of course." There is always more to learn, and each show provides you with the chance to grow as you are confronted by different problems. Dedicated professionals are needed to maintain and operate today's concert equipment. In addition to the technical knowledge required to set up, operate, and maintain the equipment, you are responsible for the well-being of everyone present. The concert production environment is potentially dangerous, and mistakes can harm the crew, the performers, or the audience. There is no room for mistakes with heavy loads suspended overhead and complex electrical equipment all around.

The larger a crew, the more complex a setup becomes. It is therefore important to work as a team. Many people are involved in concert production, and everyone must work together. Each person is as important as the next to the success of the show. The technical success of a show is as important as the performance. Without sound or lighting equipment, performers would be seen in a very different light and would not be heard at all. The technology has created the need for logical and artistic people to complement musical performances, to bridge the gap between art and science to give the audience the best possible performance.

This book is divided into two main categories: sound and lighting. Before I tackle these subjects, however, I discuss power and rigging, both of which are common to sound and lighting systems. A good understanding of power and rigging is crucial, because your life and the lives of the crew, performers, and audience may depend on it. The sections on sound and lighting explain each component of these systems and provide an overview.

The appendixes provide electrical formulas, cable wiring information, and a sample production checklist to illustrate the arrangements and checks for each performance. For this new edition, I have expanded the sections on radio microphones and digital dimmers. This new edition covers areas outside the concert touring environment in which the skills and technology developed for concert performances are being used. The book concludes with a glossary of commonly used terms and a bibliography for further reading.

Setting up and maintaining touring concert systems is not simple. I hope that this book will help workers who are starting out on the road.

ACKNOWLEDGMENTS

I wish to acknowledge all the people with whom I have worked over the past 25 years who have helped to prepare this book. I also wish to acknowledge all the people who keep the show on the road.

Line drawings, photographs, and sketches were prepared by George Gorga and Sean Hackett with contributions from Phoebus Manufacturing, Shure Microphones, Yamaha Corporation, Avolites, JBL, Rosco, Vari-Lite, Inc., and Jands Production Services. Additional photos were supplied by Heidi Duckworth. Lighting plot courtesy of Sean Hackett.

PART I

INTRODUCTION TO CONCERT SYSTEMS

CHAPTER 1

INTRODUCTION TO THE TOURING CONCERT

The need for touring concert sound and lighting systems has increased with the demand for concert tickets. Every year there is a bigger tour than the year before, with more equipment and technology, and a larger touring staff. The venues needed to accommodate elaborate productions are usually larger, and so is the audience. Touring sound and lighting systems have developed to provide the equipment necessary for performances in large arenas. At first concert tours used available equipment designed and manufactured for theater use, but as the industry grew, specific products were developed for touring concert systems. Advancements in technology from valves to transistors to silicon chips have been part of the evolution of touring systems. This evolution will continue as performers strive to present shows that surpass previous efforts.

Most touring concert equipment for major concert tours is provided by service companies that provide both sound and lighting equipment or specialize in one or the other. Selection of a particular company depends on location, performers' artistic requirements, venue size, and most important, budget. The budget usually dictates all decisions, so all too often artistic requirements are trimmed to fit financial necessities. The budget is usually determined by the popularity of the performers and their ability to attract an audience.

Various people are involved with concert production, and each has his or her part to play on the team. A production or stage manager coordinates the crew, which is broken down into sound, lighting, and performers' crew divisions.

THE TOURING PARTY: WHO'S WHO

Performers. The performers do the show, talk to the media, and encourage people to buy their records and concert tickets.

Tour manager. The tour manager oversees travel arrangements, collects money, pays bills, and addresses problems as they arise.

Production manager. The production manager oversees and arranges the technical requirements and staff for the show. These requirements are documented in the contract rider that the performers' booking agent or management company sends to the show's promoter. The production manager, who has an overview of the entire production, may have a background in sound, lighting, or stage management and can coordinate the touring and local staff.

Sound engineer. The sound engineer operates the control console and mixes the sound the audience hears. He or she also helps set up and pack the equipment.

Monitor engineer. The monitor engineer operates the monitor console, which controls the sound that the performers hear on stage. He or she also helps set up and pack the equipment.

Sound crew. The sound crew unloads, sets up, packs, and reloads the sound equipment. The crew also repairs equipment damaged in transit but usually does not perform technical repairs.

Lighting operator. The lighting operator is in artistic control of the console for the lighting system. He or she also is usually the lighting designer, who formulates the overall look of the show and selects the type, position, and color of the lighting instruments. The lighting operator also helps set up and pack the equipment.

Lighting crew. The lighting crew unloads, sets up, packs, and reloads the lighting equipment. This includes repairing equipment damaged in transit and changing burned-out gels and lamps.

Stage manager. The stage manager usually is responsible for the performers' equipment, such as drums, guitars, and keyboards. The stage manager may have assistants such as a drum crew, a keyboard crew, and a guitar crew. The stage manager may also have a specific performer's equipment to deal with, for example, guitars.

Set crew. The size of the production may call for a crew to be responsible for risers, set pieces, flooring, and props.

Truck and bus drivers. The drivers usually must drive through the night after the show has been reloaded to arrive at the next venue in time to start all over again.

LOCAL CREW

In addition to the touring crew, the size of which depends on the amount of equipment, a local crew is needed at each venue to set up and pack. The local crew is divided into the following categories:

Venue technical manager. The venue technical manager arranges the necessary local staff hired by the touring production manager and specified in the contract rider.

Loaders. The loaders unload and reload the trucks.

Stagehands. The stagehands move the equipment into position and assist the touring crew with the setup. The stagehands may be further designated into specific areas of the production, for example, sound or lighting.

Riggers. The riggers attach the chain motors used to lift the speakers and lights to the roof of the venue. The riggers may be divided into climbing and ground work.

Electrician. The electrician connects the power cables for the sound and lighting equipment to the venue electricity supply. This usually involves a three-phase connection for the lighting equipment and one connection for the sound equipment. Other services depend on the production, for example, video equipment and computerized lighting system.

Runners. The runners work under the production manager's direction as needed, for example, obtaining parts from a music store, collecting towels from the hotel, and buying batteries.

Forklift driver. The forklift driver works as directed.

Spotlight operators. Spotlight operators are needed only at showtime to operate the follow spots. Some of the follow spots may be positioned in the lighting grid above the stage, and a good head for heights is required.

House-light operators. The house-light operators switch the venue lighting on and off under the direction of the production manager.

LOCAL PERSONNEL

Additional local people employed for a concert are as follows:

Local promoter. The local promoter buys the show from the booking agent who represents the performers and sells the tickets to the show. The local promoter also ensures that the requirements set out in the contract rider are met. This includes local staff, dressing rooms, and catering.

Caterers. The caterers meet the requirements of the contract rider and ensure that crew members are well fed.

Venue staff. The venue staff needed depends on the size of venue but usually consists of ticket collectors, security personnel, ushers, parking attendants, refreshment stall operators, and program and merchandise sellers.

YOUR CAREER PATH

Being part of the touring team requires more than technical knowledge of the equipment. You must be able to work with different local people each day and to live and travel with the touring crew. Usually a bond develops among crew members as a tour progresses, and members who do not fit in usually find themselves replaced by people who do.

Working and traveling with a new challenge every day can be an enjoyable way of life. The rate of pay depends on experience, competence, and track record in the industry. A traveling allowance, called a *per diem*, is supplied. The only way to get experience and climb the ladder to a better job is to start on the road once you know how to set up the equipment.

The show must run on schedule, and the crew must be ready for work at call time. The schedule usually is worked out so that the setup can be a coordinated procedure. If people are late for their call times, the entire schedule is disrupted.

There is a career path through the ranks of a crew, from sound crew to console operator, from console operator to production manager. There also is a saying that you are only as good as your last gig, which means that if you cannot handle the heat, get out of the kitchen.

CHAPTER 2

POWER

Power must be treated with care to avoid accidents and blown fuses. A licensed electrician should connect the power to the supply.

Available power varies among countries, but it is generally a three-phase, four-wire, 50/60 cycles per second (Hz) alternating current (AC) system. Three cables carry 240/120 V, and one neutral cable has no voltage. The supply voltage is 120 V/60 Hz in the United States, 220 V/50 Hz in Europe, and 240 V/50 Hz in the United Kingdom, Australia, and New Zealand.

AC means that the voltage varies between +240/120 and −240/120 V at 50/60 times per second (50/60 Hz) (Figure 2–1).

The power source must be checked for fuse value and location. The amount of power required by the sound system depends on the number of power amplifiers being used. Allow 4 amperes (A) per power amplifier. All the amplifiers will not draw 4 A, but if the system must reproduce transient peaks, which will draw maximum power, the fuses should be capable of handling the demand. The current draw is proportional to the program being amplified.

The amount of power for the lighting system depends on the number of lamps and their wattage in use at any one time. Sometimes a lighting system may have more lamps than power available, so all the lamps cannot be on at once. The number of lamps on at any given moment must be within the capacity of the available power, or rather than a dramatic burst of light, there will be a blown fuse and a blackout.

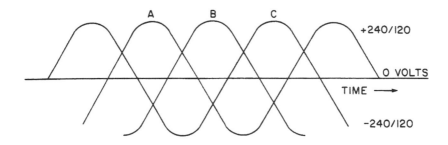

Figure 2–1.   Three-phase power. The voltage varies between +240 V/120 V and –240 V/ 120 V at 50/60 cycles per second (Hz).

Ohm's law states that current (amperes) = watts divided by volts, or power (watts) = volts multiplied by amperes.

METERING THREE-PHASE POWER

A three-phase power cable has five cores: three phases that carry the voltage, one neutral that has no voltage, and one earth.

Phase to neutral should read 240 V in the United Kingdom and 120 V in the United States. This can vary from 250/130 to 230/100 V depending on the distance from the supply transformer and the load on the supply. Phase to phase should read 415 V in the United Kingdom and 208 V in the United States. Again, this varies with the supply. Neutral to earth should read zero. There may be a trickle voltage of 10 V maximum. The neutral and earth cores are connected at the supply; this is called a *multiple earth neutral* (MEN). Phase to earth should read 240 V in the United Kingdom and 120 V in the United States. This reading determine whether there is an earth core. If there is no earth, the reading is zero.

A *transformer* is an AC device for changing AC to a higher or lower value. It consists of two separated and insulated copper wire coils wound around a common soft-iron core and arranged so that electrical lines of force around one winding pass through to the other through the iron core. There is no electrical connection in the usual sense between the two coils (Figure 2–2). One winding, called the *primary*, is connected to the power source. The other winding, the *secondary*, gives out the voltage, which depends on the number of coils. If there are 240 turns on the primary and 120 on the secondary, 240 V is reduced to 120 V. A separate coil is necessary for each phase. It is common to have several taps on the secondary to give a selection of voltages (Figure 2–3). Transformers become very hot when they are under load and should be situated in a well-ventilated area.

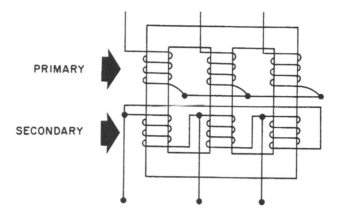

PRIMARY

SECONDARY

Figure 2–2. Three-phase transformer. No electrical connection exists between the primary and secondary transformer windings.

Figure 2–3. Three-phase transformer. These are the various taps available for a suitable secondary voltage.

LAYING POWER CABLES

Because power cables carry large currents, a magnetic field around them can cause hum in audio cables. Power cables should never be left in coils while under load because this causes inductance that results in a buildup of heat and possibly a melted cable. Power cables should cross audio cables at right angles.

CHAIN MOTOR POWER

When motor power is connected, it is important to check that the phasing is correct and the motor goes up when the up button is pressed and down when the down button is pressed. The limit switches in the motor, which stop the motor a few links from the hook, depend on the phases' being in the correct order.

SOUND-POWER DISTRIBUTION SYSTEM

A power distribution system is needed to distribute the power from the main building supply or generator. The system must be protected by fuses or breakers at each connection. If a supply fuse blows, switch off all the amplifier racks before restoring the fuse, because the surge of power may blow fuses or breakers in the distribution system. Most of the electricity goes to the power amplifiers (Figure 2–4).

LOADING A THREE-PHASE DISTRIBUTION SYSTEM

All three phases must be loaded as evenly as possible. The front of house (FOH) control, monitor system, and musicians' equipment must be on the same phase, because a fault between an instrument and sound equipment on different phases can cause a potential difference of 415/208 V, death to anyone in its path.

Power amplifiers are loaded on phases one and two, and the monitor system, instruments, and FOH control are loaded on the third phase. If a separate power source is used for the musicians' equipment, it must be checked to ensure that it is on the same phase as the monitors and FOH. A meter reading of 415/208 V measured between active-on instrument power and active-on monitor power shows that they do not share the same phase. When they are on the same phase, the reading is zero. It may be necessary to load the third phase with amplifier racks to balance the load between the phases on larger systems.

Ground loops are caused when the ground wiring of two or more components loop from one to another, either through signal cables or when the chassis of a piece of equipment finds a second ground, such as a scaffold pipe.

Figure 2–4. Sound-power distribution board. The distribution board is used to route the supplied electricity to where it is needed on the stage. Most of the electricity is needed for the power amplifiers.

The induced radio frequency and power line hum cause a hum that is amplified with the signal. Instead of going directly to earth and disappearing, the noise currents travel along paths not intended for signal and are modulated (Figure 2–5).

The likelihood of ground loops is greatly reduced with the use of balanced lines. The balanced signal line does not use the shield of the cable for

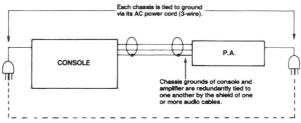

The ground path between the two AC plugs provides a redundant ground (ground loop) since the audio cable shield(s) already does the job.

A typical sound system ground loop caused by redundant audio shield and AC mains ground paths.

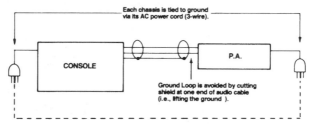

Dual ground path provided by AC cords does not create ground loop since the two chassis are not grounded redundantly via cable shield.

Elimination of the typical ground loop by cutting the shield of the audio cable retains AC safety.

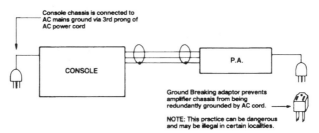

One way to eliminate ground loops is to break the AC ground on one or more pieces of sound equipment, although the practice is not recommended.

Figure 2–5.   Typical ground loops in a sound system. (Courtesy Yamaha Music.)

any signal, and the shield is not connected to main ground when it passes through the balancing transformer.

Under no circumstances should the main ground be removed from any piece of equipment—it is there to prevent potential shocks. Although removing it may appear to solve the hum, it is a potentially dangerous solution. Removing the mains ground relies on the signal cable to provide a ground, a very dangerous practice.

LIGHTING-POWER DISTRIBUTION SYSTEM

A distribution system is needed to distribute the power from the main building power supply or generator. The distribution system should isolate each dimmer rack and provide outlets for chain motor power, smoke machines, console, fans, and so on. Each point of distribution should be protected by a fuse or circuit breaker. When any connections are made, turn off the supply to the outlet being connected to avoid any arcing between plug and socket. Such arcing would burn the connectors and is extremely dangerous.

A *generator* is a diesel engine that produces electricity. Generators used for powering sound and lighting systems should be in excellent working order and capable of constantly varying loads. A generator may stall if suddenly asked to deliver maximum power in an instant if it is not running properly, the last thing anyone wants during a performance.

ELECTRICAL SAFETY

Electricity presents little risk to users when used correctly. Electric shocks caused by electrical equipment occur without warning and are often serious. Voltage any higher than 30 V can be dangerous. Circuits are constructed that dramatically increase voltages. A circuit that operates on a 12 V supply can easily generate a much higher and lethal voltage.

Electrocution is not the only risk when dealing with electricity. The risk for death from fire caused by faulty circuits and equipment is the same as, if not higher than, that for electrocution. Electrical faults are a common cause of building fires.

CHAPTER 3

RIGGING

Rigging is a specialized field that requires a great deal of practical and theoretical knowledge. A qualified rigger is legally required in most parts of the world to rig the points for attachment of the chain motors.

RIGGING OF POINTS

To rig the points in suitable positions, the rigger must first know how to make up bridles on the ground. For example, in a venue with rigging beams 15 feet apart and 60 feet above the floor and a stage 6 feet high, at least 30 feet of clearance is required between the stage and the motor hook. Under these conditions, the point must be at least 36 feet above the ground, which is 24 feet below the beams and at least 5 feet away from the nearest beam. The bridle must be made up with one 20-foot wire attached to a spanset, chain, or wire to wrap around the roof beam and a 15-foot wire, again with a spanset, chain, or wire to wrap the beam. At the point where the 20-foot wire and 15-foot wire meet, the chain motor hook attaches. At the end of each wire should be a bow shackle. A third bow shackle joins the motor hook onto the wires (Figure 3–1).

It is vital to check all rigging equipment thoroughly before it is used. As the wires are hoisted into the roof, they must be checked to ensure that they are sitting correctly in the shackles. Wire ropes should be checked for any broken strands, because once one strand goes, the rest can easily follow. Do not use kinked wires. Do not use any piece of rigging equipment that does not

Figure 3–1.   A bridled point. Bridling often is necessary to place the points in optimum position.

look up to par. Hessian sacks can be used to protect slings from the rough edges of roof beams.

The desired position of the point should be chalked on the floor as a circle with an X in it about a foot wide, making it easy for the riggers to see it from the roof. It is far easier to use points with a straight drop than it is to rig bridled points. Reeving (choking) a sling around an object with one eye through the other halves the safe working load of the sling (Figure 3–2).

CHAIN MOTORS

The chains on the motors must be inspected every time they are rigged. Two-ton motors must be checked for any twisted links by means of running the block the entire length of the chain. The chain can easily become twisted in transit, and when the motor is taken to its maximum height, a twisted link can jam or shear with disastrous results. A twisted chain increases friction as it passes through the block.

The most fragile part of the chain motor is the contactor, which switches the motor on and off. The terminals of the contactor can be burned through continual clicking on and off, so it is advisable to keep the motor going once it is under load. The power supply for the chain motors must be phased correctly so that the motor moves up when the up button is depressed. If the phasing is incorrect, the safety-limit switches in the motor will not work. The

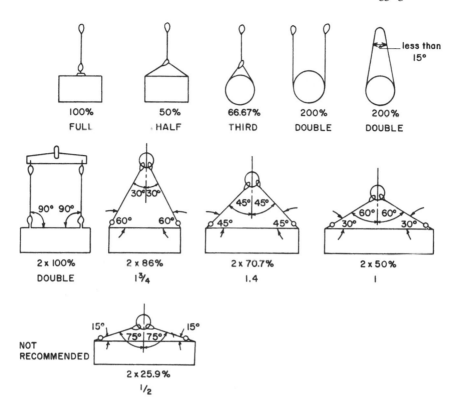

Figure 3–2. Methods of slinging. These are variations in the loads imposed on slings. (Courtesy Department of Industrial Relations of New South Wales.)

limit switches are set to make sure that the motor does not run into the hook but stops a few links from it.

The person operating the motors must ensure that no one is standing under a load being raised or lowered. Common sense must be of paramount concern, because taking chances with rigging is taking chances with lives. Also, learn how to tie knots correctly (Figure 3–3).

Wire ropes should be color coded for length so that each sling can be readily identified (Figure 3–4). It is important to understand the safe working load of wire rope slings for various applications (Figure 3–5).

Spansets, made from loops of nylon, are color coded for safe working load (Figure 3–6). Because they are lightweight, spansets have many advantages over chains or wire ropes, but unlike chains and wire ropes, spansets are not fire resistant, necessitating additional care.

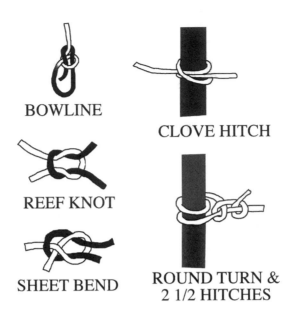

BOWLINE

CLOVE HITCH

REEF KNOT

SHEET BEND

ROUND TURN &
2 1/2 HITCHES

Figure 3–3.   Useful knots. Learn how to tie knots correctly, or have someone experienced tie them. Do not take chances. (Courtesy of Sean Hackett.)

RED	=	5 FEET
WHITE	=	IO FEET
BLUE	=	20 FEET

Figure 3–4.   Wire-rope color code. Wires are color coded so that their length can be easily identified for quick and efficient setup.

SAFE LOADS OF STEEL WIRE ROPE SLINGS
WIRE ROPE OF G1570 GRADE

Rope Diameter	SINGLE SLING OR SNOTTER	NIP OR REEVABLE SLING — SQUARED LOADS	NIP OR REEVABLE SLING — ROUND LOADS	2 LEG SLINGS AND UNEQUALLY LOADED 3 OR 4 LEG SLINGS — 30°	60°	90°	4 LEG SLING - Flexible Loads Only
mm			Safe Working Load—Kilograms or Tonnes				
6 x 24 (15/9/F) FIBRE CORE							
5	220	110	160	420	380	310	620
6	320	160	240	620	550	450	900
7	440	220	330	850	760	620	1.2
8	580	290	430	1.1	1.0	820	1.6
9	730	360	540	1.4	1.2	1.0	2.0
10	900	450	670	1.7	1.5	1.2	2.5
11	1.1	540	810	2.1	1.9	1.5	3.0
12	1.3	650	970	2.5	2.2	1.8	3.6
13	1.5	750	1.1	2.9	2.6	2.1	4.2
14	1.8	880	1.3	3.4	3.0	2.5	5.0
16	2.3	1.1	1.7	4.4	4.0	3.2	6.5
18	2.9	1.4	2.2	5.6	5.0	4.1	8.2
20	3.6	1.8	2.7	6.9	6.2	5.0	10.1
22	4.3	2.2	3.2	8.3	7.5	6.1	12.2
24	5.2	2.6	3.9	10.0	8.9	7.3	14.5
26	6.0	3.0	4.5	11.7	10.4	8.5	17.0
28	7.0	3.5	5.3	13.6	12.1	9.9	19.8
32	9.2	4.6	6.9	17.7	15.9	12.9	25.8
6 x 37 (18/12/6/1) FIBRE CORE							
36	12.2	6.1	9.1	23.5	21.1	17.2	34.4
40	15.1	7.5	11.3	29.1	26.1	21.2	42.5
44	18.2	9.1	13.6	35.1	31.4	25.6	51.2
48	21.8	10.9	16.3	42.0	37.7	30.7	61.5
52	25.4	12.7	19.0	49.0	43.9	35.8	71.5
56	29.5	14.7	22.1	57.0	51.0	41.5	83.0
60	34.6	17.3	25.9	66.8	60.0	48.8	97.5
Load factor	1.0	0.5	0.75	1.93	1.73	1.41	2.82

Note: Safe Loads for *Heavy Duty or Rough Usage* shall be reduced to 4/5ths of the above values.

A handy rule to remember—To find the Safe Load of a Wire Rope (in kilograms)—Used as a Single Sling: Square the rope diameter and multiply by 8.

Example—20 mm diameter rope. Safe Load is 20 x 20 x 8 = 3200 kg = 3.2 tonne.

This table is based on Regulation 144 (2) of the Construction Safety Act and Australian Standard AS 1666–1976.

Figure 3–5. Safe loads of steel wire rope slings. Reductions in capacity depend on application. Divide kilograms by 0.45 to find pounds; divide millimeters by 25 to find inches. (Courtesy Department of Industrial Relations of New South Wales.)

VIOLET	=	1 TON
GREEN	=	2 TON
LIME	=	3 TON

Figure 3–6.   Spanset color code. Spansets are color coded for load capacity. This capacity is reduced depending on the method of slinging.

PART II

SOUND SYSTEMS

CHAPTER 4

SPEAKER SYSTEMS

Several different types of speaker systems are in use, each with its own characteristics that must be taken into consideration during flying and stacking. Environment dictates how the speakers should be used to obtain the best results. Sometimes it may be necessary to get as much power from the speakers as possible by taking advantage of acoustic coupling. Other situations may require maximum dispersion of the cabinets. A cabinet's dispersion characteristics are normally governed by the dispersion characteristics of the mid- and high-frequency bands because the lower frequencies are omnidirectional.

TYPES OF SPEAKERS

A multitude of speaker cabinets are designed for all types of sound reinforcement. The most common types of cabinets for concert sound reinforcement are three-way active cabinets. Each cabinet is divided into three distinct parts that are driven by different signals, as follows:

1. *Low band*. The low band of the cabinet is for the lower frequencies, typically 0 to 250 Hz. The designs of the low chambers vary a great deal; 18- or 15-inch speakers are loaded in either a folded horn or reflex ported design.
2. *Mid band*. The range of the mid band varies among cabinets. Some cabinets have a front-loaded horn design or infinite baffle; others have a front-loaded horn with phase plugs. Mid speakers are either 10 or 12 inches,

and they cover frequency ranges from 250 to 1,200 Hz. Cabinets with phase plugs have a wider frequency response, anywhere up to 4,000 Hz.

3. *High band.* The components that cover the higher frequencies are horns with compression drivers. The compression drivers use an alloy or titanium diaphragm to provide fidelity and extended high-frequency response. The frequency range of the high-band section depends on the crossover point of the mid band. The high band generally runs from mid-band crossover frequency all the way up. Exceptions have tweeters for the ultrahigh frequencies.

In addition to three-way active cabinets, sub-low cabinets sometimes are used. Their frequency range is generally 0 to 63 Hz.

STACKING SPEAKERS

Speakers should be situated to provide good, even coverage to the audience with minimum obstruction. When stacking a speaker system, make sure the deck is solid and level. Often a scaffold that appears to be solid and level sinks or bends with the concentrated weight of a speaker system, causing the speaker stack to lean. The scaffolding should be inspected before, during, and after stacking to ensure safety. Speaker stacks for outdoor concerts must be secured so that they cannot blow over. Sub-low cabinets should be stacked directly on the floor so that the cabinet can couple with the ground. Other speaker cabinets should be above head height so that the sound from the cabinets can disperse.

FLYING SPEAKERS

Speakers are flown to provide wide coverage with no sight-line obstructions in arena-style venues. Speakers also are flown to provide front-row sound for people seated in the balconies. Most modern speaker cabinet designs incorporate flying hardware. Positioning cabinets in a flown array depends on where people are seated (Figure 4–1).

DELAY SYSTEMS

Use

Delay systems are used to maintain clarity and level over a large area. Although a large number of cabinets can be used for power, clarity is lost after a certain distance. In indoor venues where there is a great deal of reverberation, the reverberant signal may make the amplified signal unintelligible in the higher frequencies, necessitating additional horns to maintain clarity.

Figure 4–1. Flown speakers. Speakers are flown to provide wide coverage with no sight-line obstruction.

The delay system must blend in with the sound from the main system and not sound like a separate system. The audience should hear only a loud and clear sound that appears to come from the stage area.

Setting Delay Time

The equation for setting the amount of delay time in a delay system is the distance in meters divided by 340 and multiplied by 1,000, which equals time in milliseconds. Measure the response of the main system at the delay system position first, then tune the delay system to bring up the overall response to equal that of the main system. Often this means that minimal or low frequencies are not needed. The average speed of sound is 340 meters per second, which increases with heat and humidity. The actual speed depends on atmospheric pressure and air density, so the equation provides only a rough estimate. Once the rough time is set, it can be tuned exactly with a pulse, that is, a single click; the time can be set so that the click appears to come from the main speaker stacks.

CENTER CLUSTERS

Center clusters sometimes are flown between stereo clusters to achieve powerful, even coverage of a venue. A center cluster can be used exclusively for vocals so that the audience hears the voices as coming from between the stereo clusters.

DISTRIBUTED SYSTEMS

A distributed system is used for low-level amplification to a large number of people. The distributed sources of sound should be placed at specified distances and on the same arc so that they can share a common signal, which is delayed for each arc of cabinets. Every source of sound requires individual level control so that it can be adjusted to suit the surrounding area. This can be done by means of adjusting either the amplifiers or the relevant crossovers.

ANALYZING SPEAKER SYSTEMS

A spectrum analyzer is used to measure the entire spectrum of sound as a person hears it and displays it on a series of light-emitting diodes (LEDs) that match the layout of a graphic equalizer. Analyzer response must be set to suit each application. For reading a musical program, fast attack and slow decay are suitable; for acoustic measurements with pink noise, slow attack and slow decay are best. Divisions of the audio spectrum are shown in Figure 4–2.

Pink Noise

To measure the performance of a speaker system with an analyzer, a source of sound, pink noise, is required. *Pink noise* is noise with equal amounts of energy in all frequencies that has been passed through a filter to bring the energy to the level heard by the human ear (Figures 4–3 to 4–8).

Using the Analyzer

Sound varies among the thousands of seats in an auditorium. The speakers should be positioned to give as uniform a response as possible, and the crossovers should be set before the equalizer is touched. To analyze the speaker system without room interference, the measurement microphone should be positioned one and one-half times the height of the speaker stack, although sometimes this is not practical. Most clubs and concert halls have a very live sound because their large number of reflective surfaces improves room gain. In large halls this gain can be as much as 30 dB but is not uniform. The high frequencies are attenuated more than the low frequencies by molecular air

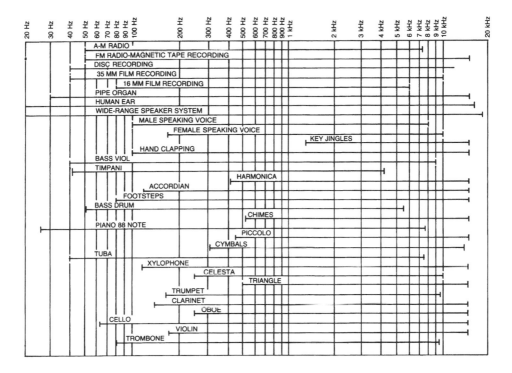

Figure 4–2.   Divisions of the audio spectrum.

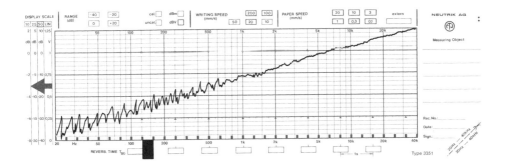

Figure 4–3.   White noise. White noise has equal energy in each frequency band according to a linear scale and therefore has a rising response on a logarithmic scale.

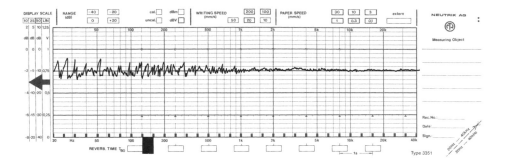

Figure 4–4. Pink noise. Pink noise has a flat response when the spectrum is divided according to the way the ear hears (logarithmically) and is therefore used in acoustic measurements.

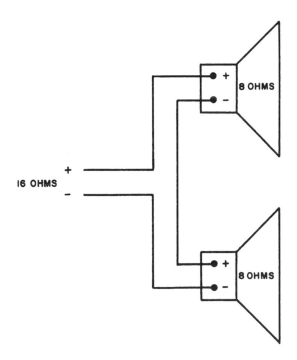

Figure 4–5. Speakers wired in series. Speakers and drivers arc-wired in series to match impedance to the type of amplifier being used.

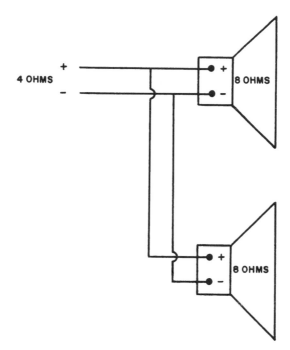

Figure 4–6. Speakers wired in parallel. Speakers and drivers are wired in parallel to match impedance to the type of amplifier being used. In some cases, two pairs of speakers are wired in series, and each pair is wired in parallel to match the impedance for optimum use of available amplifier power.

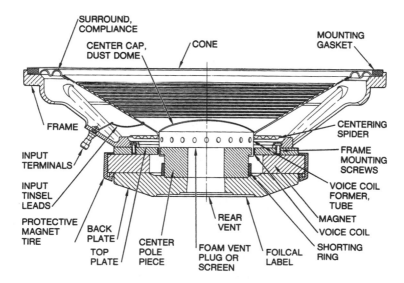

Figure 4–7. Cross section of a speaker shows arrangement of speaker parts. (Courtesy JBL Professional.)

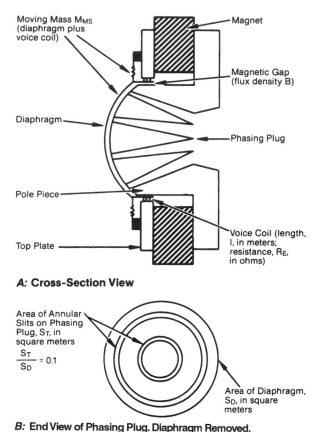

Figure 4–8. Cross section of a compression driver shows arrangement of high-frequency horn driver parts. (Courtesy JBL Professional.)

absorption. Analyzing at the back wall naturally shows a loss of high frequencies, and trying to equalize them back in would make the sound painful everywhere else in the room. The initial measurement should be near and in front of the speaker stack and then at various positions in the room to give an overall view of the necessary adjustments that must be made (Figure 4–9).

Some hints for using an analyzer are as follows:

1. Try to maintain the average curve of equalization around the zero mark, and generally cut obtrusive peaks rather than boost all others to preserve headroom in the system.
2. In stereo systems, no matter how much equalization is needed, avoid boosting a particular frequency or band of frequencies on one channel and cutting the same frequencies on the other channel. No matter how much the frequency response has improved, a considerable phase shift has been introduced that will create a noticeable image shift.

Figure 4–9. Spectrum analyzer. This unit is used to measure the entire spectrum of sound as one hears it and displays it on a series of LEDs.

3. Try to avoid sharp response changes. Compromise by setting one frequency at 0 and the adjacent frequencies at –2 rather than at +2 and –4. Carry a tape of a piece of music you know well and use this as the final judge of the system's response to the music.

If you are equalizing a room and the analyzer shows marked deviation from flat (more than 5 dB), moving the speakers or the listening position may be the answer rather than destroying the overall equipment response. The measurement microphone may have ended up at a node or antinode, that is, at a point of minimum or maximum pressure at a low frequency. The measurement microphone sums the acoustic energy from the speakers and the reflected sound from the room surfaces. That summation can cause a peak or a dip through cancellation, and the resultant curve is a disaster. Fortunately the ear is not as clinical as the analyzer and generally misses the aberrations in sound that it does not want to hear. Set the analyzer to an intelligent compromise between what the analyzer says and what the ear wants to hear.

For one-night gigs, in which time is limited, place the measuring microphone in a central position and put the pink noise through each stack and through a check at the mixing position. The farther back you go, the more reverberation and less direct sound you receive. A drop in high frequencies due to absorption and a huge rise in lower frequencies from the back wall also occur. Take all these variables into account when selecting a mixing position. Finally, after equalizing for a flat response, make subtle changes to make it sound right—music is highly subjective, and spectrum analyzers do not always share your taste.

CHAPTER 5

POWER AMPLIFIERS

The input for power amplifiers comes from the mixing console, usually through graphic equalizers, crossovers, and limiters. This signal is amplified to drive the speakers. All power amplifiers perform the same function but have different power capacities and features, such as visual output displays and ampere status warnings for shorts or direct current (DC) voltage on the output. The input voltage of an amplifier varies between 1 and 1.75 V root mean square (RMS). The maximum input voltage must be applied to the input to achieve maximum amplifier power. Amplifier output requires a heavy-duty cable to deliver the signal to the speakers. The cable must be capable of taking high currents to ensure a minimum of voltage drop and full power to the speakers. The harder an amplifier works, the hotter it becomes, and cooling is thus critical. Dust buildup in an amplifier restricts airflow and causes the amplifier to overheat. Amplifiers with thermal protection switch off, but those without protection develop faults. Figure 5–1 shows an amplifier with its lid removed.

PATCHING AMPLIFIER RACKS

Most power amplifiers have two channels, a left and a right. To drive three-way active speaker systems, the amplifiers should be installed in racks to minimize the wiring needed to connect them to the input signals, the power supply, and the speakers. The input signal assigned to an amplifier determines

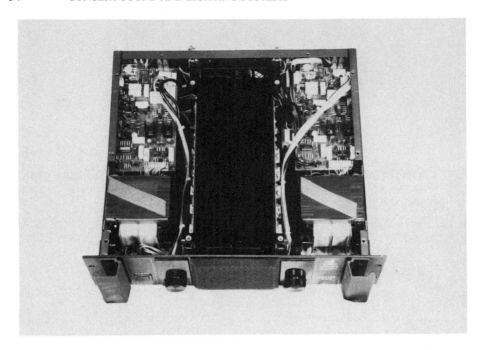

Figure 5–1.   Amplifier with lid removed. Many different power amplifiers are available.

the speaker component connected to the output. Signal and speaker cables are coded with numbers: 1, low; 2, mid; 3, high. The number of speaker components connected to an amplifier channel depends on the electrical resistance (ohms) of the speaker components and the way they are wired.

Speakers can be wired in series or parallel (see Figures 4–5 and 4–6). The total resistance of speakers wired in series is calculated by summing the values of the speakers. A speaker cabinet with two 8-ohm speakers wired in series would put a load of 16 ohms on an amplifier. The resistance of speakers wired in parallel is a little more difficult to calculate. The values of the speakers are multiplied and the total is divided by the sum of the values. A cabinet with two 8-ohm speakers wired in parallel would put a load of 4 ohms on an amplifier ($8 \times 8 = 64$; $64 \div 16 = 4$). The amount of power that an amplifier delivers depends on output load. The lower the speakers' resistance (ohms), the higher the output power (watts), and the greater the amplifier's power, the cleaner is the sound.

A rack of four two-channel amplifiers used to drive four speaker cabinets assigns four channels to low frequencies, and each channel drives a 4-ohm load (two 8-ohm speakers wired in parallel). Two channels are assigned to drive the mid-range speaker components (a 4-ohm load). Each amplifier channel assigned to mid-range components drives two cabinets, each containing two 16-ohm speakers wired in parallel (8 ohms). Connecting the two cabinets in parallel reduces the load to 4 ohms. The high frequencies are reproduced by compression drivers, typically 16 ohms, with two in parallel for an 8-ohm load. Compression drivers are designed to reproduce only the higher frequencies, and low-frequency signals quickly destroy the diaphragm of a compression driver. High-frequency drivers do not require as much power as speakers for the lower frequencies. Two drivers on each amplifier channel with a load of 8 ohms reduce amplifier output power (Figure 5–2).

Power amplifiers usually are set with the volume full up; most level adjustments are made by the electronics controlling the system. Certain cabinets may have to be turned down with the volume controls on the amplifiers. The amplifiers are the last components to be switched on in the signal path and the first to be switched off, because any electronics in the chain that are powered up while connected in line will cause a loud, possibly damaging click through the speakers (Figure 5–3).

Figure 5–2.   Racks of amplifiers. Amplifiers are installed in racks to minimize the wiring necessary to connect them.

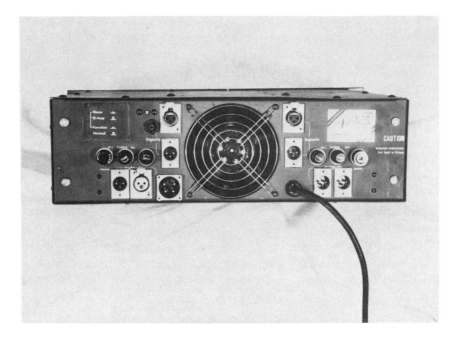

Figure 5–3.   Rear panel of an amplifier.

FAULT FINDING

There is a checking procedure for isolating a problem in a system and determining whether a speaker component or an amplifier is faulty:

First, disconnect the speaker cable. Test the speaker cable with the known working amplifier channel, making sure the amplifier channel is turned down when you are connecting and disconnecting speakers. If the speaker is faulty, the amplifier may have gone DC. Check amplifier fuses and replace if blown. Do not reconnect the speaker cable yet. If the fuse has blown with no load attached to the output, the amplifier has probably blown power transistors and may therefore produce a DC output. If an amplifier goes DC, it means that the rail voltage of approximately 90 V DC goes straight to the output. This voltage destroys speakers. A reading of more than 0.5 V DC on the output of an amplifier indicates it has gone DC. Some amplifiers have a DC protection circuit that disconnects the output if a DC voltage appears at the output. Finally, if the amplifier requires repair by a technician, the rack may be repatched to accommodate all the components by connecting all four high-frequency drivers into one channel. The now-available channel can be repatched with the input and output from the faulty channel.

TURN ON–TURN OFF PROCEDURE

The correct turn on and turn off procedure is as follows. First, check that volume controls are down and amplifiers are switched off. Turn on power to the rack. Check whether the rack fans are on. Some amplifiers are built with fans, and others need fans installed in the racks to keep them cool. Turn on the amplifier power switch and check whether the amplifier fans are working. Finally, turn up the volume controls. Check each signal and amplifier channel to isolate any problems.

CHAPTER 6

MULTICORE SYSTEM

Multicore cables are used to distribute the microphone input lines and the crossover outputs to desired points in the sound system. These cables are called *snakes, trunks,* or more commonly *multicores*.

SIGNAL DISTRIBUTION

The microphone inputs are plugged into an input box that connects to a splitter, in which each line is split to two different outputs. One output connects to the front of house (FOH) console, the other to the monitor console (Figure 6–1). The cables used to connect the microphone inputs to the FOH console are tinned copper pairs, each pair individually shielded with aluminum-polyester and stranded tinned copper drain wire. The most common cable used is Belden 8769 with 19 pairs or 8773 with 27 pairs. Various connectors are available to connect the multiway cables to the input box, splitter box, and consoles. All multipin connectors are delicate and must be handled with extreme care. Each connector has a locating arrangement that allows it to mate in one way only. Forcing the connection can damage the connectors and pins. The most suitable type of pins are gold coated and do not tarnish (Figures 6–1 and 6–2).

When a microphone is connected to the FOH console and the monitor console through the multicore system, it lowers the input gain. If the line is disconnected from one of the consoles, gain increases to the console that

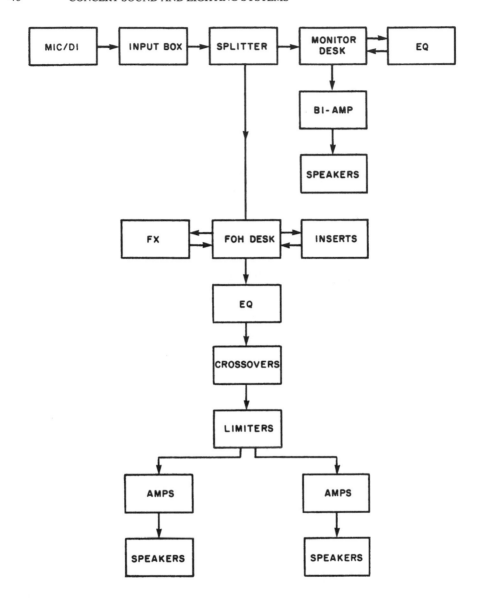

Figure 6–1. Sound system signal path.

remains connected. Condenser microphones and direct boxes, which require phantom power, should not be disconnected when their control channels are on, because this causes a loud click that can damage the speaker system. Before any microphones or direct boxes are connected, both consoles should have the relevant channels muted. Separate multicore cables should be used

Figure 6–2. Multiway input box. This box terminates the multiway cable to a series of connectors that accept the signal inputs, such as microphones and direct boxes.

to distribute the crossover outputs to the amplifiers to reduce the possibility of cross talk between the low-level microphone inputs and the high-level crossover outputs. The cable most commonly used is Belden 8778, which has six pairs individually shielded.

SPLITTER SYSTEMS

Splitter boxes can be fitted with transformers to isolate the FOH and monitor consoles and provide an isolated split for a mobile recording facility. Phantom power does not pass through an audio transformer. Some splitter systems use transformers to isolate the FOH and monitor consoles to eliminate interference between consoles and minimize gain reduction. These systems do not pass phantom power and require an external source of phantom power for condenser microphones and direct boxes. Transformer splitter systems designed for use with mobile recording facilities use the transformers to isolate the signal sent to the recording facility, which allows the FOH and monitor consoles to be unaffected by the console in the recording facility (Figures 6–3 and 6–4).

Figure 6–3. Multiway splitter box. These boxes are sometimes fitted with transformers to isolate the front of house and monitor consoles and provide an isolated split for a mobile recording.

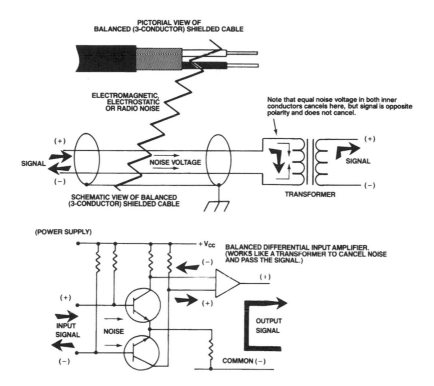

Figure 6–4. Noise rejection in a balanced line. The radio frequency interference cuts across both conductors, inducing equal voltages in the same direction. These voltages "meet" in the differential amplifier (or transformer) and cancel out. The signals generated by the microphone flow in opposite directions in each conductor and do not cancel out. Theoretically, in a perfectly balanced system, only the desired signal gets through the differential amplifier or transformer. (Courtesy Yamaha Music.)

CHAPTER 7

DRIVE SYSTEM

The drive system consists of the audio components in the audio chain, which drive the amplifiers once the signal has left the mixing console (Figure 7–1).

GRAPHIC EQUALIZER

The graphic equalizer consists of 27 potentiometers (pots) or faders that are on third-octave centers from 40 to 16,000 Hz (16 kHz). These controls enable the sound system to be tuned to suit a given environment. Tuning is a subjective operation that requires considerable experience and skill. Listen closely to any equalizing with an analyzer and let your ears be the final judge. Each side of a stereo sound system requires a graphic equalizer, and it is the first component in the drive chain (Figure 7–2). A digital graphic equalizer offers the facility to store and recall settings. The use of digital equalizers makes the process of system equalization more efficient by allowing quick comparisons between settings.

CROSSOVERS

The crossover, or frequency dividing system, divides the signal into two, three, or four separate bandwidths. The crossover allows control of the level fed to the amplifiers that drive the low frequencies, mid frequencies, and high frequencies, respectively. A fourth bandwidth may be acquired for sub-low

Figure 7–1.   Drive rack.

octaves. The crossover frequencies depend on the type of speaker system. The slope between each frequency band at the crossover point is generally 24 dB per octave.

The crossover points on a three-way active speaker system with additional sub-low cabinets would have the following bandwidths:

1. Sub-low cabinets, 20 to 63 Hz. The sub-low cabinets can be used as part of the entire speaker system and tuned with the other frequency bands or used independently with signal fed from an auxiliary send from the mixing console. When the sub-low cabinets are used as part of the entire speaker system, some crossover units feed a mono sum of the left and right stereo inputs.
2. Low-frequency bandwidth, 20 to 250 Hz.

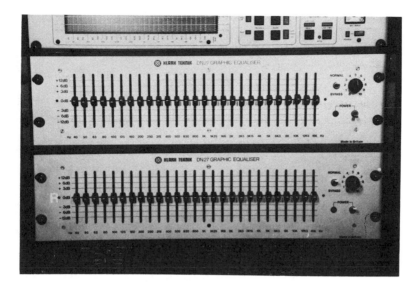

Figure 7–2. Graphic equalizer. This piece of equipment enables tuning of the sound system to suit the environment.

3. Mid-frequency bandwidth, 250 to 1,200 Hz. The mid-frequency band varies depending on the type of mid-range cabinets. The range of the mid band may vary between 250 and 1,000 Hz to 250 and 4,000 Hz.
4. High-frequency bandwidth, 1,200 Hz and up. The crossover point of the mid range determines the high-frequency crossover point.

Some crossover units have phase correction and can correct phase errors that occur in the loudspeakers and cabinets. Phase alignment should begin at the highest-frequency band. All other frequency bands should be adjusted in sequence from highest to lowest. If after an initial adjustment further adjustments are needed on any frequency band, all lower bands require adjustment to compensate. To set phase alignment accurately, use an analyzer to provide a pictorial view of the crossover regions and set phase controls for the flattest response. A sine wave from a signal generator at each crossover point can be used. Alter the phase control for minimum volume, then switch the polarity switch to invert one of the outputs to achieve true summation (Figure 7–3).

Some crossovers also feature time alignment, which delays some bandwidths to keep the source from all bandwidths the same.

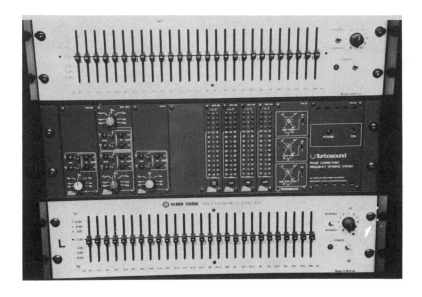

Figure 7–3.   Crossovers divide the signal into two, three, or four separate bandwidths.

LIMITERS

After the signal leaves the crossover it passes through a limiter, a device that limits the amount of signal reaching the amplifiers to avoid distortion or damage. The threshold of the limiter is set to the input voltage of the amplifiers being driven. The ratio should be infinite for maximum protection. Some crossovers are equipped with limiters inserted halfway through the filter network to avoid frequency shifting problems associated with the more normal end of line limiting.

DRIVE MULTICORE CABLES

Drive multicore cables distribute the outputs of the drive system to the amplifiers. Figure 7–4 shows the rear of a drive rack. Generally there is a multicore cable for each side of a stereo system. Because all the multiway cables are strapped together, the drive cables end up on one side of the system, usually on the basis of where the monitor console is situated. A cross-stage drive cable distributes the signal to the amplifiers on the opposite side. The common standard of drive-cable color coding is white for the left side and red for the right side.

Figure 7–4.   Rear of a drive rack. Drive cables connect to the rack with multipin connectors.

CHAPTER 8

HOUSE MIXING CONSOLES

The several different types of front of house (FOH) mixing consoles all perform the same basic function to control the level, tone, and output designation of all console inputs (microphones, effects, tapes) and follow similar signal paths. The more sophisticated a console, the more functions it can perform and the more facilities it has available for complex applications (Figure 8–1).

INPUT CHANNEL

The following is a step-by-step explanation of all functions on an input channel in the order the signal follows.

INPUT

The input is connected through an XLR female socket on the rear panel of most consoles. This can be a microphone or direct box connected to a multicore line, tape machine, or effect return.

MICROPHONE OR LINE SWITCH

This switch selects between a low-impedance input such as a microphone or direct box and a high-level, line-level input such as a tape machine or effect return.

Figure 8–1.   Input module of a front of house console. (Courtesy Yamaha Music.)

Input Gain

Input gain controls the amount of level a channel accepts. These controls can be a fully variable pot or a switch with several fixed values.

Pad

The pad alters input gain but only by specific amounts. It is used in conjunction with the input gain control for precise adjustments.

Phase Reverse Switch

The phase reverse switch reverses input polarity, a feature useful for correcting the phase cancellation caused when two microphones are very close.

Group Select Switches

The group select switches assign channel output to the group-mixing buses or directly to the main stereo output.

Equalizer Section

The equalizer section controls channel tone. The two types of equalization are *peaking* and *shelving*.

PEAKING.
Select the center frequency and cut or boost the Q (bandwidth), which is either fixed or variable, around the selected frequency. A frequency of 1,600 Hz allows gain control of higher and lower frequencies. The bandwidth between the lowest and the highest frequency can be adjusted on some consoles from a broad band to a narrow band. Parametric equalizers provide control of the bandwidth.

SHELVING.
The frequency selected determines the point at which everything above or below it will be cut or boosted. A low shelf (160 Hz) allows all frequencies below 160 Hz to be cut or boosted. A high shelf (5 kHz) allows all the frequencies above 5 kHz to be cut or boosted.

High-pass Filter

The high-pass filter allows all frequencies above the filter frequency to pass and attenuates all frequencies below it. The amount of attenuation usually is between 12 and 18 dB per octave. Use high-pass filters to reduce the rumble picked up on stage that discolors the desired sound.

Equalizer On and Off

Some consoles have a switch to bypass the equalizer for comparison before and after equalization.

Insert Point

The insert point in the channel, normally after the equalizer and before the fader, is where limiters, noise gates, or other devices are inserted into the channel through insert jack sockets mounted on the rear panel above the input or on jack fields on the front of the console.

Auxiliary Sends

Auxiliary sends often are labeled *echo send* or *foldback send* and provide discrete outputs from the channel. Some consoles have a switch to designate the send either *prefader*, whereby the control operates independently of the fader, or *postfader*, whereby the output depends on the fader. Auxiliary sends can be used for effects sends, sub–low cabinet sends, and monitor sends back to the stage, among other things.

Pan Pot

Pan controls select channel position in the left and right dimensions for stereo application. The pan pot also is used to assign mono groups on some consoles.

Prefade Listen Switch

Prefade listen (PFL), also called *cue* or *solo*, selects the channel to the headphone output and cue meter. This allows you to listen to that particular channel independently of the fader.

Phantom Power

The phantom power switch supplies 48 V to power condenser microphones and direct boxes. The 48 V flows down both balanced audio lines, that is, pins one and two; zero reference is at the shield of the cable (pin one). Phantom power does not pass through a transformer. A reading of 48 V between pins one and two and between pins one and three is needed if phantom power is to power microphones and direct boxes.

Mute Switch

The mute switch turns on the channel. The PFL function still operates with the channel off on most consoles.

Fader

The fader sets the level sent to the channel's output to assigned groups and the auxiliary sends switched to the postfade position.

Voltage-controlled Amplifier Controls

Voltage-controlled amplifiers (VCAs) allow gain to be adjusted with external DC voltage. They are more useful than faders are because the audio signal can go directly to the main outputs, shortening the path of the signal through the mixer and reducing the risk for signal degradation. The VCA controls look like those of faders except that the DC control voltage, not the signal, passes through the control. Grouping channels with the VCA master controls allows the level of the assigned channels to be adjusted without any accumulated noise. Because the VCA master controls only signal level, not signal destination, the channel must be assigned through the group select switches.

Mute Assign

A mute assign switch allows a master switch to mute groups of channels assigned to a mute master.

OUTPUT

The output section provides master level control for groups, auxiliary sends, and VCA masters (Figure 8–2).

The matrix allows the different console outputs to be grouped as required to provide the desired balance. Several matrix outputs are available for different combinations for different destinations, that is, main stereo speaker systems, delay systems, center fills, and tape machines. Auxiliary returns accept the signal from line-level units, effects, and tape players.

TALKBACK MODULE

The talkback module, which differs on all consoles and may have some or all features, can contain an oscillator for calibrating the console and the entire sound system. It also may have a switch and microphone input that can be assigned to all the groups and to the talkback output, which can be connected to the monitor console to feed through the monitors for on-stage instruction for equipment and sound checks. Some modules have a feature for intercom, headphones, and microphone systems for communicating with the stage (Figures 8–3 and 8–4).

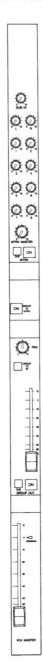

Figure 8–2.   Master module of a front of house console. (Courtesy Yamaha Music.)

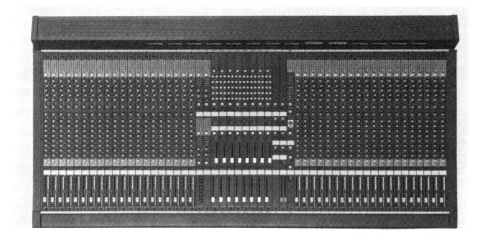

Figure 8–3.   Front of house console. The many different types of front of house consoles all perform the same basic functions. (Courtesy Yamaha Music.)

Figure 8–4.   Rear panel of a front of house console. All connections to the console are made in the rear panel. (Courtesy Yamaha Music.)

POWER SUPPLY

The power supply for the mixing console usually is a separate unit. This keeps the transformers, which convert AC input into DC voltages to drive the electronics, away from the console. The normal voltages supplied to the console from the power supply are + and –18 to 20 V to drive the electronics, 48 V for the phantom power, and additional voltage for meter lamps, console lamps, and VCA control (Figure 8–5).

GAIN STRUCTURE

The gain structure (Figure 8–6) is the relations among all the components in the signal chain. It should be set so that the console output, graphic equalizers, and crossovers correspond. Do this by using a tone to set channel input level, crossover levels, and amplifier levels to zero. What the output meters show on the console is exactly what amplifier output will be. The best way to run the console is to have adequate headroom available for transient peaks without residual noise. An input signal that is too high distorts both channel

Figure 8–5.   Mixer power supply. This usually is a separate unit from the mixer. (Courtesy Yamaha Music.)

and console output, affecting all input. The input must be set to a reasonable level with the input attenuator. It is pointless to turn down the crossovers or amplifiers if the console is overloading. Instead, have some headroom on the system and keep the console input gains down. Leave enough headroom for live music, because transient peaks need room to move to avoid distortion, blown components, and generally bad sound.

CONSOLE CARE

Consoles must be kept clean with regular dusting; accumulation of dust destroys console components. Never use spray cleaners. Pots and faders can become noisy if they become dusty or dirty. Spray cleaners only exacerbate the problem by removing their lubricating film along with the dust. Cover a console when it is not in use to reduce its exposure to dust.

MIXING

Mixing is not something to learn from a book. Although you must understand the equipment being used, the room acoustics, and the material being performed, mixing is an art that builds on knowledge and experience. There are a number of steps to take to keep the sound system under control and sounding good.

Most important is gain structure. Ease your way into a mix; do not start with everything running flat out. Be careful to retain enough headroom for soloists and vocalists. Always start the sound check with the rhythm section, then check the melody instruments, and then the vocalists and soloists. Build the mix on the foundation of the rhythm. It is pointless to have the drums and bass so loud they drown out everything else.

Try to keep the sound dynamic so that it has some life and is not just a wall of noise. It should be possible to pick out each instrument and differentiate it from others being played. Beware of overequalizing, or you will end up trying to tune each instrument to fit in with others rather than letting them fit in naturally. If a drum keeps ringing, no matter what you do with the equalizer, the answer may be to have the drum tuned properly or move the microphone. The drum tone may have the same frequency as a resonant frequency in the room.

Check all microphone positions before starting a sound check to correct, if necessary, microphone position, proximity to other microphones, source of the sound being miked, and fittings and stands.

Make effects complement the music, not confuse it. Subtle reverberations can enhance the sound, and loud repeats can be used for dramatic effects.

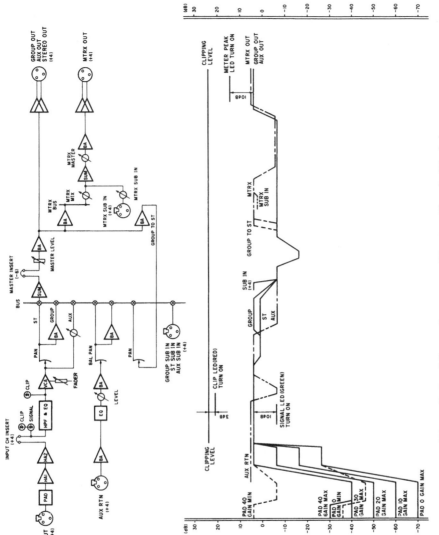

Figure 8-6. Mixer gain structure. (Courtesy Yamaha Music.)

The level of the sound depends on the type of music, the environment, and the available power. A highly reverberant room, in which all the low frequencies are subject to large amounts of room gain and the higher frequencies are absorbed, requires a different approach than an open field or a room with minimal reverberation.

CHAPTER 9

EFFECTS UNITS

A multitude of different effects units are available. Most of them are digital delays or reverberation units. Effects for live performances either reproduce the sound of the performer's recording or complement the performance creatively. Echoes, or separately identifiable repeats, should blend in with the music and not sound like an electronic malfunction. Figure 9–1 shows an effects rack.

DIGITAL DELAYS

The digital delay is a device that uses digital technology to store an audio signal and play it back. The digital delay has evolved from the tape echo, which had difficulty maintaining signal quality. Digital delays store the signal by means of digital sampling, a technique that samples the sound several thousand times a second and converts it into a binary code that is stored in the unit's memory. The more memory available in a unit, the better is the frequency response and the longer the delay. The advantage of digital storage is that it turns the sound into numbers. Digital storage maintains excellent frequency response and provides options to modify the stored sound, including flanging, phasing, pitch change, echo, and chorus effects.

63

Figure 9–1.   Effects rack. Live effects are used to reproduce the sound of the performer's recordings or to complement it.

REVERBERATION UNITS

Reverberation units store information the same way digital delays do but build several different delays to produce reverberation. The more sophisticated a reverberation unit, the more intricate the reflections can be to simulate acoustic environments that probably could not be found in reality. Reverberation units have a standard set of programmed room sizes, but these can be altered to produce a particular effect.

MUSICAL INSTRUMENT DIGITAL INTERFACE

The musical instrument digital interface (MIDI) system is a language that sends and receives information between digital instruments and effects units.

Sixteen channels send and receive information in each MIDI cable. MIDI is a hexadecimal message sent as a series of bytes. Two types of messages are sent—status and data bytes. *Status bytes* represent the type of message, and *data bytes* represent the action to be carried out. A MIDI controller connected to several effects units can be programmed to change programs at the touch of a button. The most practical way to operate effects for live performances is to give each song, or if necessary each part of a song, a program number.

USE OF EFFECTS

Study the instruction manual for the digital effects. The first step to understanding a unit is to know how to store and recall programs. With that knowledge, you can explore the vast capacity of these units to mix in stereo.

CHAPTER 10

INSERTS

Units inserted in the audio chain to modify or control the signal are called *inserts*. Most consoles have insert points for each channel, subgroup master, auxiliary outputs, and main outputs. Inserts can be *equalizers* if more equalization is required than available on the console; *noise gates* for reducing spill from other instruments or residual noise from direct sources; or *limiters* for controlling the level or producing compression effects. The two most common inserts are limiters and noise gates (Figure 10–1).

LIMITERS

Limiters fix a ceiling of maximum level without changing the dynamic range below the threshold. The amount of gain reduction depends on the ratio control setting, which can vary from no compression to infinite compression at the threshold. The level at which compression begins is set by the threshold control. An output level control can adjust the overall gain. Compression is the process of reducing dynamic range; a compressed signal has a higher average level.

To smooth out variations in microphone level, use a low compression (2:1). To smooth out variations in instrument level, use a 4:1 ratio. Smooth a bass sound by lessening the variations between the strings and increasing the sustain. To raise a signal out of a mix, apply compression and raise the level. The compressed signal will have a reduced dynamic range and a higher

Figure 10–1.   Insert rack. The two most common units inserted are limiters-compressors and noise gates.

average level. To protect the speakers, the limiter ratio should be infinite and the threshold set at the input voltage of the amplifier.

NOISE GATES

Noise gates are used to control the point at which a channel is on when the gate is open to keep residual unwanted background noise from being amplified. The channel remains off until a certain input level is achieved. The amount of signal gated is a function of both ratio and threshold. The attenuation limit sets the desired amount of noise suppression. Attack and release control the speed of attenuation. *Attack* applies to the signal heard as it comes out of the noise gating mode. *Release* governs the time for the signal to die away once the gate is shut. Noise gates can be operated by means of an external source that switches the gate on when an external signal is applied through the key connector. Some gates switch on once a signal has reached a certain level and then remain on, even if the signal falls below the threshold.

A quick setup procedure for noise gates is as follows. Set ratio and attenuation limit to the maximum. Set attack and release controls to the fastest positions. Listen to the signal. Set the threshold for the desired cutoff point. Adjust the ratio to achieve the desired rate of signal decay. Use the attack and release controls to set the smoothness of attenuation. Finally, set the attenuation limit control for the desired amount of noise to be suppressed.

CHAPTER 11

MONITOR SYSTEMS

The monitor system enables each musician to hear what the other musicians are doing. The difference between a front of house (FOH) mix and a monitor mix is that the FOH mix usually is a stereo output to the left and right speaker stacks and the monitor mix is customized for each musician. The monitor mix provides information that allows each musician to stay in time and in tune. Sometimes, however, musicians become carried away with their monitor requirements and end up wanting a fully mixed version of the group with their own contribution the loudest.

Monitor mixing is much more complex than FOH mixing, because each mix output must be individually mixed and listened to on its own at the side of the stage. This can be confusing because it may sound dreadful alone but be just what is needed on stage. It is important to listen continually to the mixes and watch the musicians closely. The monitor operator is the person on whom the group depends to combine all the individual efforts on stage into a complementary whole. The monitor operator must walk around the stage at sound checks and listen to how each mix contributes to overall sound.

MONITOR CONSOLES

Monitor consoles (Figure 11–1) differ from house mixing consoles in number of outputs. A monitor console may have up to 16 outputs, each channel having a level control for each output. A 32 into 12 console has 32 input channels

Figure 11–1.   Monitor console. These consoles differ from house mixing consoles in their number of outputs. (Courtesy Yamaha Music.)

and 12 outputs. Graphic equalizers (Figure 11–2) are inserted across the outputs to equalize each cabinet driven by each mix. The graphics are inserted rather than patched in the chain so that the monitor operator hears what is coming from the speaker after it has been equalized. It is important to know exactly which outputs are close to feedback, so they can be quickly adjusted if feedback starts. There is nothing more annoying when listening to or performing music to hear feedback screeching through the speakers.

Tuning the monitor system depends on the position and musical content of the monitor speaker. A wedge monitor with only vocals can have the lower frequencies rolled off to reduce the amount of rumble. A monitor cabinet for a drummer requires fatter sound with a different sort of tuning. Do not overequalize and end up hacking the sound to pieces. Of course you will hear feedback if you cover the end of the microphone or point it into the cabinet, but that does not happen during a performance. Always discuss a monitor mix with the musicians before plowing into it. No matter the level at which you start, musicians invariably want more, not less, which leaves you no headroom and on the brink of feedback. Musicians sometimes must compromise (for example, the singers need more vocal so the guitar player must make do with less), so the monitor operator must use tact in suggesting necessary changes.

Figure 11–2. Equalizer rack. Graphic equalizers are inserted across each output to equalize each cabinet driven by each mix.

MONITOR SPEAKERS

The main type of monitor cabinet is the *wedge monitor,* so called because it is wedge shaped. Wedges may contain a number of different components, such as two 12-inch speakers and a compression driver and one 15-inch speaker and a compression driver, or vice versa. These cabinets can be run with passive crossovers or biamplified and run two-way. The crossover point is related to the type of component. Side-fill cabinets placed on either side of the stage are more substantial than wedges. Drum and keyboard monitor cabinets usually must handle more power and lower frequencies than wedges can handle.

IN-EAR MONITORS

The use of in-ear monitoring systems is becoming more common. They allow consistent monitoring night after night, no matter what the situation. In-ear monitors are not a cure-all for monitoring woes. They present a new series of challenges for monitor engineers. Ear monitors can reduce ear fatigue by reducing exposure to excessive levels, but they can be dangerous if not properly protected. Brick wall limiting should be used to provide protection from unexpected feedback from on-stage wedges or electronic failures. In-ear monitors give the engineer greater control of the sound mix and better sound quality, and they decrease risk for feedback. The performer has greater freedom of movement and reduced ear and vocal fatigue.

MIX CONTENTS

Each monitor mix depends on the musicians, their music, and the size of the stage. A monitor system schematic is shown in Figure 11–3. An eight-send monitor system for a group of musicians consisting of drummer, keyboard player, saxophone player, guitarist, bass player, and lead vocalist would typically consist of the following:

Mix 1: Side-fill stage right. This mix would have a general balance of drums, vocals, and possibly some instruments.

Mix 2: Side-fill stage left. This mix is similar to mix 1.

Mix 3: Lead vocalist. A pair of wedges for the lead vocalist would contain the lead vocal, snare drum, and melody instrument.

Mix 4: Guitar player. This mix would contain only the guitar player's vocal, and most of the information required would come through the side fill.

Mix 5: Bass player. This mix would contain only the bass player's vocal, and most of the information would come through the side fill.

Mix 6: Keyboard player. The keyboard player would need snare, vocals, and other instruments.

Mix 7: Saxophone player. The saxophone player would need the saxophone and other instruments depending on his or her position on stage.

Mix 8: Drums. The drum monitor would contain the drums, bass guitar, and vocals.

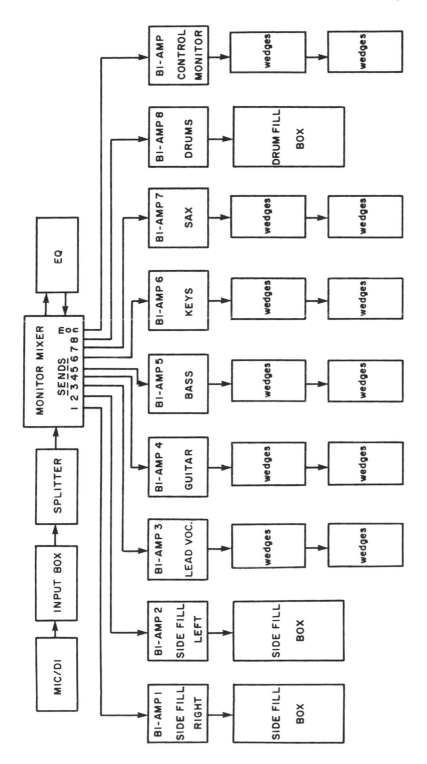

Figure 11–3. Schematic of monitor system.

CHAPTER 12

MICROPHONES AND DIRECT BOXES

Microphones convert acoustical energy into electrical energy.

TYPES OF MICROPHONES

A *dynamic microphone* has a diaphragm in a strong magnetic field. Sound waves that strike the surface of the microphone cause the coil to move in the magnetic field. The movement generates a voltage that corresponds to the sound pressure on the surface of the diaphragm.

A *condenser microphone* (Figure 12–1) involves electrostatic principles rather than the electromagnetic principles of a dynamic microphone. A condenser microphone has a diaphragm placed adjacent to a backplate, and capacitance varies with sound pressure. Condenser microphones sometimes require a pad between the diaphragm and the microphone preamplifier.

A *C-ducer microphone* is a sensing tape with preamplifier and power supply. Because the C-ducer is flexible, it can be affixed to the curved surfaces of instruments such as a harp or guitar (Figure 12–2).

A *ribbon microphone* has a thin metal ribbon suspended between the poles of a magnet to sense sound pressure.

A *pressure zone microphone* (PZM) uses the pressure zone at an acoustical boundary to eliminate distortion problems common with other microphones. The active element in a PZM is a pressure-calibrated electret capsule mounted so that it faces the boundary and lies within the pressure zone. All incoming sound is received indirectly, free of distortion caused by phase interference (Figure 12–3).

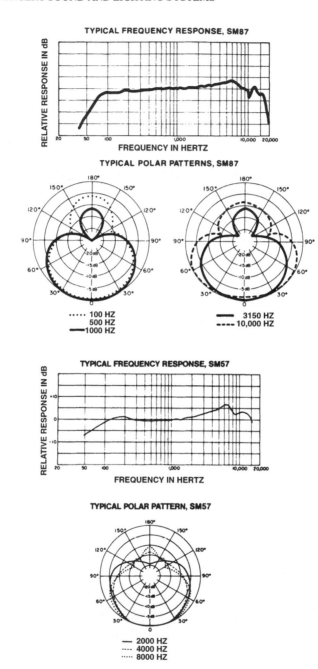

Figure 12–1.   Microphone patterns. (Courtesy Shure Bros.)

Figure 12–2.   Microphones on a drum kit.

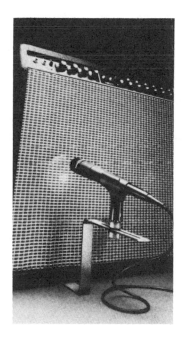

Figure 12–3.   Microphone on an amplifier. (Courtesy Shure Bros.)

A hypercardioid lavaliere microphone, an *Isomax microphone* is extremely small and can be positioned in otherwise inaccessible areas.

A *radio microphone,* which incorporates a standard microphone into a radio transmitter, has limiters between the microphone and the transmitter to keep the signal from overloading the transmitter. Developments with wireless systems have given performers the opportunity to be considerably more mobile than with hard-wired microphones and at an affordable price. The use of a multiple radio microphones is becoming more common; multichannel systems with antenna distribution are used.

A wireless microphone consists of three main components: an input source, a transmitter, and a receiver. The size of antennas is directly related to the wavelength (and inversely proportional to frequency). Lower radio frequencies require larger antennas; higher frequencies require smaller antennas. Antennas should be maintained to achieve maximum performance from the system line of sight between transmitter and receiver. The distance between transmitter and receiver should be kept to a minimum. It is preferable to use long audio cables to get the signal from the receiver to the sound system than to transmit over long distances or use long antenna cables.

DIRECT BOXES

The *direct box,* also known as a DI (direct injection), matches the impedance of an instrument to the input impedance of a mixing console. An active direct box has a transformer and a circuit powered by batteries or the phantom power supply. A passive direct box has only a transformer and provides no boosting for low-level signals. The direct box can be connected to any high-impedance instrument such as an electrical bass or synthesizer. Some instruments provide a balance-line output for direct connection to mixing consoles (Figure 12–4).

MICROPHONE PLACEMENT

For live concerts most microphones are positioned as close to the source as possible. The closer the microphone, the stronger is the signal, the less spill there is from other instruments, and the less chance there is of feedback. Microphone stands should be as rigid as possible so that they do not stray from the set position. Condenser microphones are more delicate than dynamic microphones, but all must be treated with care to maintain their quality (Figure 12–5).

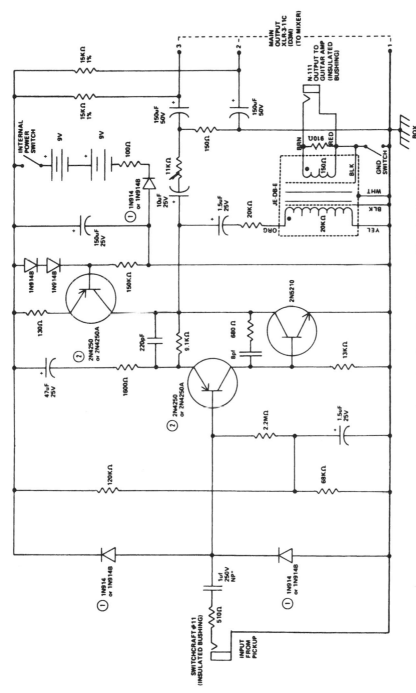

Figure 12–4.   Schematic of an active direct box. (Courtesy Yamaha Music.)

```
                          Microphone Plot

CONCERT:              ALLSTARS              VENUE/DATE: APOLLO
```

Lne #	Channel Name	FOH Chnl	Mon. Chnl	Mic.Type	Stand
1	KICK	1	1	RE-20	S/B
2	SNARE TOP	2	2	SM 57	S/B
3	SNARE BOTTOM	3	3	SM 57	S/B
4	HI HAT	4	4	C-951-CK1	S/B
5	RACK TOM 1	5	5	MD 421	M/B
6	RACK TOM 2	6	6	MD 421	M/B
7	RACK TOM 3	7	7	MD 421	M/B
8	FLOOR TOM 1	8	8	MD 421	S/B
9	FLOOR TOM 2	9	9	MD 421	S/B
10	O/H - LEFT	10	10	C-414	L/B
11	O/H - RIGHT	11	11	C-414	L/B
12	SIMMONS - LEFT	12	12	DIRECT	—
13	SIMMONS - RIGHT	13	13	DIRECT	—
14	BASS DIRECT	14	14	DI	—
15	BASS MIC	15	15	RE-20	S/B
16	GTR - LEFT	16	16	SM 57	S/B
17	GTR - RIGHT	17	17	SM 57	S/B
18	CP-70 PIANO	18	18	DIRECT	—
19	DX-7 LEFT	19	19	DI	—
20	DX-7 RIGHT	20	20	DI	—
21	KURTZWEILL - A	21	21	DIRECT	—
22	KURTZWEILL - B	22	22	DIRECT	—
23	CONGAS -LEFT	23	23	MD 441	M/B
24	CONGAS -RIGHT	24	24	MD 441	M/B
25	BACKING VOCAL 1	25	25	SM 58	L/B
26	BACKING VOCAL 2	26	26	SM 58	L/B
27	BASS VOCAL	27	27	SM 58	L/B
28	GTR VOCAL	28	28	SM 58	L/B
29	¢ VOCAL	29	29	SM 58	STRAIGHT
30	SPARE VOCAL	30	30	SM 58	STRAIGHT

KEY
S/B - SMALL BOOM
M/B - MEDIUM BOOM
L/B - LARGE BOOM

Figure 12–5. Microphone patching list. The patching list identifies input location and designation, type of microphone, microphone stand, and any additional electronics to be patched into the channels of the front of house and monitor consoles.

CHAPTER 13

SOUND SYSTEM
SETUP PROCEDURE

PREPARATION

The difference between various pieces of sound equipment assembled in the same room and a *sound system* is the operator's speed of assembly, ability to set up and operate a series of shows on schedule, and ability to rectify faults. Touring sound systems need constant maintenance to give optimum performance.

It is essential to be prepared so that equipment can be set up quickly and efficiently on site. A sound system list is a good idea (Figure 13–1). The setup must be coordinated with lighting and other production staff so that workers are not tripping over each other and making the task of setting up a show a nightmare. Call times are necessary for setup, sound check, and show so that all crew members arrive on time and keep to a schedule.

First establish the type and number of speaker cabinets and their stacking or hanging configuration. Knowing the number of speaker cabinets allows you to identify the amplifiers, speaker cables, and rigging hardware needed. The equipment should be color coded as follows to identify its desired location at the venue:

Red: Stage left (public address system [PA] right)

Yellow: Stage right (PA left)

Green: Front of house (FOH)

Orange: On stage

CONCERT PRODUCTIONS

ENGINEER	DATE OUT	DATE IN	ARTIST:	SUB HIRES	NO.OF CASES	CUBIC METRE
F.O.H.MIXER(S)						
F.O.H.DRIVE						
F.O.H.EFFECTS						
F.O.H.ACC.CASE						
MONITOR MIXER						
MONITOR E.Q.						
MON.ACC.CASE						
MON.SPEAKERS						
MON.POWER AMPS						
MON.SPKR.CABLES						
PWR.DIST.BOARD						
3 PHASE CABLES						
240 VOLT CABLES						
MICROPHONES						
MIC.STANDS						
MIC.CABLES						
MULTICORE						
SYSTEM SPARES						
SPKR.SPARES						
FOH.SPEAKERS						
FOH.PWR.AMPS						
FOH.SPKR CABLES						
CHAIN MOTORS						
RIGGING						
FLYBELTS						
EXTRAS						

Figure 13–1. Sound system list. Adequate preparation ensures smooth setup.

Use of colored tape or stickers facilitates locating the equipment. If the same equipment is used for a series of shows at different venues, the color code sends the same cabinets, amplifiers, and speaker cables to the same side each time, making it easier to identify any faults.

The number of wedge cabinets, side fills, and drum monitors determines the number of amplifiers and the number and type of speaker cables and crossovers. Check the console, graphic equalizers, and crossovers to ensure that all components function correctly.

The FOH control equipment can be lined up and marked with the channel assignment, and the gain structure can be set between console and drive electronics.

The power distribution system must be capable of handling the amount of amplifier racks being used. Have spare fuses handy so that you can replace a blown fuse quickly without interrupting a scheduled sound check or performance.

Microphone lists can be drawn up with the multicore and monitor console numbers. The FOH and monitor consoles often do not have the same channels patched in the same order. Mark the multicore numbers above the inputs of the monitor console so that the inputs can be patched automatically.

The more careful the preparation, the smoother is the setup. Because unforeseen problems often occur, it is important to have spare time in which to address them. The sound equipment should be assembled as quickly as possible so that any running repairs do not delay scheduled sound checks or rehearsals. A delayed sound check can disrupt many schedules.

For outdoor concerts, carry enough weatherproofing to cover the equipment. Tie down any speakers stacked outdoors with ropes or cargo straps.

Before attempting to load a truck, determine how many cases are the same size so that you may stack them in blocks. Pack all the larger, heavier cases on the bottom and the light ones on top. Load in logical order so that power cases, rigging cases, and chain motors end up at the rear of the truck and can come off the truck first to facilitate setting up. Mark the weight of each case on the top and bottom to avoid accidents. Because most damage to equipment sustained transit is caused by vibration in the truck, load the cases as tightly together as possible and tie them with ropes or straps. Other transit damage occurs during loading and unloading, so everyone must be careful

SETUP

Do the following to get the sound system out of the truck, set up, packed, and reloaded. The more equipment and the more crew on a show, the more complex setup becomes. It is necessary to define crew members' areas of responsibility, because many of the setup steps can be done simultaneously.

Unloading the Truck

One member of the sound crew should stay in the truck to ensure that each case is leaving the truck with enough people (Figure 13–2). The other members of the sound crew should direct the cases to their destination in the venue and begin setting up. Color coding allows for a minimum of direction.

Rigging

Chalk the position of the points on the floor clearly and correctly so that the riggers can see them clearly from the ceiling. This eliminates the need for shouting.

Motors should be positioned and all necessary rigging attached to the hook (wire rope bridles and spansets to wrap around the ceiling beams). Check two-ton motors for any twisted links by running the block the length of the chain. The block can easily become twisted in transit, and a twisted link can jam in the motor or the block. If a motor is rigged with a twisted link, the situation can be remedied by means of passing the motor between the two chains before attaching any load to the hoist.

Figure 13–2. Unloading the truck. One member of the sound crew should stay in the truck to ensure that the stagehands are handling cases properly.

Check the motor power to ensure that the phasing is correct and that the motor moves up when the up button is pressed and down when the down button is depressed. Only one member of the crew should operate the motors (Figure 13–3). If the phasing is incorrect, the safety switches in the motor do not function. The motor control cables can be attached to the bar that holds the speakers (the bumper) and loomed together. The best position from which to operate the hoists is in the center between the left and right clusters. As each motor is connected to the motor control box, label it so that when it is disconnected and reconnected you do not have to move the motors to identify them. Motor 1 should be the motor closest to the center of the stage, motor 2 the next one, and so on. Each side of the speaker system has the same motor numbers starting in the center and moving outward all the way around to the cable pick.

Figure 13–3.   Rigging. Only one member of the crew should operate the motors.

POWER CONNECTION

The venue electrician normally makes the three-phase power connection (Figure 13–4). You must check this service before turning on the power. Have the connection double-checked by the FOH and monitor engineers. If any trouble occurs during the show, the FOH engineer will be too far away to deal with a power failure; the monitor engineer therefore must know what to do if the power fails.

Establish the location and rating of the fuses (or breakers). Access to the fuses or breakers is crucial in the event of faults. The power distribution cables can be run out to where the power amplifiers will be situated. At outdoor concerts all power connections must be weatherproofed. Connections

Figure 13–4.   Power connection. The venue electrician normally makes the three-phase power connection.

should never be directly on the ground but must be strung up on the scaffolding or placed inside a case. It is not good enough to wrap plastic around the connection. Heavy dew also can cause a short in power cables left exposed overnight.

HANGING THE SPEAKERS

As soon as the bumper is lifted, it is time to attach the speaker cabinets. While the points are being rigged, which often takes longer than you want, the speaker cables can be attached to the bumper and all the cabinets lined up in the correct order ready to be attached.

The speaker cables must be coded and a plot drawn up so that each cabinet can be easily identified through its cable number (Figure 13–5). The cables should be patched into the amplifier racks so that they are in series horizontally to enable lower cabinets to be turned down, if necessary, without affecting the higher rows. Of course there are exceptions to this practice. When the cabinets are attached to the bumper, their angles must be checked to ensure that they cover the proper venue areas. The speaker cables should be pulled out of sight lines so that they do not block the view of people sitting at the sides of the stage. It is often impossible, however, to keep the view totally clear for everyone.

Stacking Speakers

Before attempting to stack speaker cabinets, make sure that the scaffold or deck that will support them is flat and capable of taking the weight. Check the scaffold during and after stacking. The weight of the speakers may force the foundations down into soft ground, and scaffold pipes may bend if not strengthened properly.

The higher and heavier a stack, the harder it can fall. If the deck is uneven to start with, the higher the stack goes, the more it will lean, which can be very dangerous. At outdoor concerts the speakers must be tied down during stacking, because a gust of wind may blow over a column of cabinets. The enemies of outdoor concerts are wind and rain, and often they come together. The best form of defense is to be prepared. Tarpaulins tied to the top of speaker stacks must be able to drain any water immediately, because a tarp full of water can easily pull down the entire stack. Keep the cabinets tied down until it is time to unstack them.

Flying Speakers

Once all speakers and speaker cables are attached, all cabinets are at the correct angles, and all rigging is firmly attached, the bumpers can be raised. The

Figure 13–5.   Hanging the speakers. Speaker cables must be coded and a plot drawn up so that each cabinet can be easily identified through its cable number.

person operating the chain motors must make sure that no one is standing under them when they are moving. The bumpers should be as level as possible before being moved up to trim height. Although all the motors should move at the same speed, they do not, so when the bumpers are at trim height they should be leveled with only one person instructing the operator. Use the motor code to identify the motors for clear instructions. The motors must be watched continuously while they are moving. If one motor stops, for whatever reason, the other motors will become overloaded, with disastrous results. Motors can stop because a contact breaks in the motor or a control cable snags. A motor can become overloaded if the bumper is not level and too much weight is transferred to the other motor, although the motors are protected by an overload clutch. In short, raising and lowering the chain motors is a task that requires complete concentration.

Amplifers

Amplifiers must be positioned in well-ventilated, accessible areas. Amplifier racks with fans that blow air front to back should be placed in rows back to back so that the fans are not blowing hot air out the back of one rack and straight into the front of another one (Figure 13–6). Racks that draw the air in the back and also out the back should be placed in a U shape if they do not fit in a row. At outdoor concerts the amplifiers must be protected from the sun and rain but still need room to breathe. At outdoor concerts the amplifiers usually must work hard as engineers battle with the wind trying to get the sound to the audience. Signal assignment must be checked to be sure that the correct signal is being sent to the speaker cabinets; for example, horns do not last long with low frequencies. The power for the amplifier racks supplied from the power distribution system should be evenly allocated over the three phases. The FOH control equipment, monitor system, and stage instruments all must share the same phase.

Front of House Control Equipment

The multicore cables must be run out to where the mixer will be positioned. Before running them, check the route so that the cables do not pass through heavily trafficked areas or across fire exits. Cables running through public areas must be covered and secured to the floor. Multicore connectors should

Figure 13–6.   Amplifiers must be positioned in well-ventilated, accessible areas.

never be dragged along the ground. Before setting the mixer, check that the position does not violate any local laws, does not obstruct the view of the stage from seats behind the console, and is suitable for controlling the sound system (Figure 13–7). Specific seats often are held for the mixing positions, and these can sometimes be reshuffled to accommodate sound requirements.

Connect the mixer, drive rack, and effects rack and then the multicore cables and power. Turn on the system. Set the gain so that the console and crossovers are running evenly. Set a substantial show-level signal to check each amplifier channel. When the amplifier channels are being turned up, the person in control of the FOH equipment must listen for distortion. When all amplifier channels have been checked and all cabinets are functioning, the system can be tuned. After tuning from the control position, walk around the venue to check for even coverage. Any offensive area can be trimmed by means of turning down specific amplifiers.

After tuning and trimming, check the effects units, microphone set, and microphone inputs and inserts. Coordinate the microphone line check with the monitor engineer, and use a talk-to-stage microphone to direct the person

Figure 13–7. Front of house control position. Before setting the mixer, check that the position does not violate any local laws or obstruct the view of the stage from seats behind.

in charge of input source. This person should carry a spare microphone and spare microphone cables so that any faults can be quickly determined and rectified.

Monitor System

The monitor system can be set as soon as the lighting rig is raised and the stage is clear. Often it is possible to set the monitor control area before the lights are raised. When tuning the monitors, establish the threshold of feedback so that it can be quickly controlled during the show. All cables running around the stage should be laid flat and taped down so people cannot trip over them during the show.

Miking Up

Before the microphones are set, place them on their stands, per the microphone list, and position the input boxes. Once the instruments are set, the microphones can be positioned and connected to the input boxes. Miking up should be a joint sound crew effort. Patching microphone cables on your own is very time consuming because the input boxes are usually tucked out of sight. When all the microphones are set, it is time for the line check. Microphones are delicate and must be treated with care, especially the highly sensitive condenser microphones.

Sound Check

Once everything is working, a sound check can begin. When a suitable balance has been established at the FOH control position, check the coverage around the venue for any anomalies. The sound check should start with the rhythm section and proceed to the melody section and vocalists. Sometimes it is better to have the band start with the monitor system and settle on the sound on stage before the main speaker system is turned on. The sound check should conclude with the first song to be performed that night so that all the settings on the console are ready for that particular piece of music.

After Sound Check

After the sound check for the main artist, reset the consoles for the opening act. The settings on the consoles should be recorded or marked before they are tampered with. Keep the amount of resetting to a minimum. By the time the consoles are marked for the opening act, the stage should be ready to be remiked. Team effort makes this a straightforward process. Often an opening act is not as prepared as you would like, so sound checks can turn into debugging sessions or even rehearsals. These kinds of opening acts need assistance and direction. Finally, all interval tapes and disks should be cued up and ready for show time.

SHOW TIME

The sound check sets the balance to suit the room while it is empty. The sound changes when the audience is seated, as does the temperature. Monitor the gain structure of the system regularly so that it maintains its optimum performance. If the system has been lined up properly, the engineer can see at a glance the headroom available or whether there is an excessive level. Conduct a line check between any microphone repatches for opening acts. Microphone cables that must be repatched during changeovers between acts should be clearly marked so that they can be patched correctly in the difficult environment of a show.

The pressure is on to be ready for show time, and with people rushing around the stage, moving equipment, and a screaming audience, mistakes can be easily made. To avoid these mistakes, which usually take far too long to rectify, make sure there is enough light to see the markings on the cables and carry a flashlight to be sure. Mark microphone stands for their assigned positions and input numbers. Because a mispatched microphone is an engineer's nightmare, keep a spare microphone, stand, and cable near the monitor console for speedy replacement if needed. If a singer handles the microphone roughly, place a spare microphone on stage so that he or she can switch to the spare immediately.

LOAD OUT

Load out basically is the reverse of setup, only much quicker. First pack the microphones, then the mixing consoles and electronics. Loom the cables together to make packing easier. Make sure that multicore connectors are protected and not dragged along the ground. Once everything is loaded, an "idiot check" of the venue ensures that nothing has been left behind.

DIVISION OF DUTIES

Division of duties changes with the requirements of each show, number of cabinets, number of acts, and performance schedule. To maintain teamwork, duties are divided between the two main sound crew members—the FOH engineer and the monitor engineer.

The typical responsibilities of an FOH engineer are the FOH control equipment, multicore system, rigging and motors, speaker system, and amplifiers. The responsibilities of the monitor engineer usually are the monitor system, power system, microphones, microphone stands and cables, speaker system, and amplifiers.

The speaker system is the FOH engineer's prime responsibility. Additional crew members assist with it and with the amplifiers, microphones, stands, and cables when necessary. The duties remain the same whatever the size of the crew, and the sound crew must always load and unload the sound equipment.

On a concert tour with a vast amount of equipment, the sound crew must give clear instructions to the stagehands and loaders and supervise loading and unloading. If the equipment has been marked with a location code, it is sent automatically to the desired point. Work out truck-loading plans *before* it is time to load the truck and tape them to the wall of the truck.

SYSTEM CHECK

The system check procedure includes attention to the power connection, power supply, mixing console, drive system, each amplifier channel, each speaker cabinet, monitor system, and all microphone lines. The power supply must be checked before any equipment is connected.

Conduct on-site maintenance whenever possible to keep abreast of minor problems. Faulty cables and microphones should be clearly marked and their ends taped over. Spare cables, diaphragms, speakers, and castors should be part of the system. Keep a record of repairs so that recurring faults can be identified. If a compression driver blows a diaphragm every second or third show, for example, the driver may be cracked and out of alignment, which becomes very costly. The date the diaphragm is changed should be recorded for this reason.

LIGHTING SYSTEMS

CHAPTER 14

TRUSSES AND GRIDS

RIGGING TRUSSES AND GRIDS

A variety of methods are used to join truss sections: nuts and bolts, pins, and Camlocs. No matter what method is used, check each connection before the truss is lifted (Figure 14–1). The correct position to sling the chain motor is about one-fifth the length of the truss from the end. The length of the truss should be capable of supporting the load suspended without any deflection. Different types of trussing have different load capacities. The longer a truss, the more support it requires. One cannot lengthen a truss and increase the distance between the motors without reducing the load capacity of the truss.

A series of trusses connected together and lifted on several motors is called a *grid*. The number of motors used on a grid depends on the load. As a rule, support all cross-stage trusses with a pair of motors. Trusses longer than 40 feet may need an additional motor in the center depending on the load. Trusses supported by three motors must have motor tension checked so that the center motor does not end up taking most of the load. The function of the center motor is to provide additional support and reduce the amount of bounce in a truss.

GROUND SUPPORTS

When no suitable flying facilities are available, ground supports on a solid, level surface must be used. It is dangerous to lift a grid on ground supports

Figure 14–1.   Rigging a truss. Various methods are used to join truss sections such as nuts and bolts, pins, and Camlocs.

because the grid may twist if the supports are not raised together. If the supports are not raised together, one of the supports ends up taking more of the load, which can be disastrous. The heaviest part of a grid is the corner where the cables drop, and this corner becomes heavier the higher it is raised. Trusses supported on ground supports should not be climbed on; focusing should be done from a ladder.

LIFTING GRIDS

Before lifting a grid, check all the lamps for tightness and anything attached to the grid for safety (Figure 14–2). The motor controller should clearly identify where the motors are connected. A grid with a large number of looms requires a cable pick to relieve some of its load. When the grid is being raised, the cable pick also should be raised.

Once the grid is at the desired height, it must be leveled. Do not rely on line of sight. Use trim chains or a tape measure for accurate trimming. It is easy to make trim chains with lightweight chain and to tag their length, usually between 18 and 25 feet. Each motor can be adjusted so that the grid ends up perfectly level. If the grid is not leveled correctly, unnecessary strain is placed on the trussing, which can fracture the welding and cause an accident.

Figure 14–2.   Raising the grid. Before lifting a grid, check all lamps for tightness and check anything attached to the grid for safety.

CHAPTER 15

LAMPS

Lamp is the general term for an incandescent light source. A number of lamps are available to provide a wide range of wattage at different voltages (Figure 15–1).

The intensity of a light is determined by the throw, the distance from the light source to the object it is lighting. The intensity is governed by the inverse square law. Once a beam leaves a light, the area illuminated by the beam increases the farther it throws, and the same quantity of light must illuminate a larger area. If the distance between a light and the stage is doubled, the intensity is reduced to one-fourth the original.

TYPES OF INSTRUMENTS

Par cans hold par 64 bulbs and raylight kits. The 64 refers to the diameter of the bulb in eighths of an inch. The par lamp is a tungsten-halogen (quartz) lamp with a parabolic aluminized reflector that forms part of the bulb. Par cans can be bolted onto bars, typically with six lamps, which are wired to a multiway connector. Lamp 1 on a multiway bar is the lamp closest to the connector. Par bulbs also can be used as floor lamps in short-nose cans. The only adjustment available on a par can is left-right and up-down. The bulb can be turned in the can to change the direction of the beam. When the filament is vertical, the beam is wider than when the filament is horizontal (Figure 15–2).

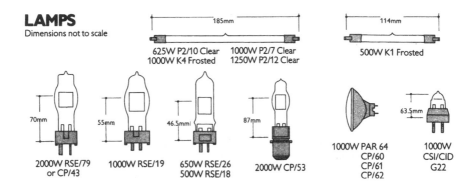

LAMPS
Dimensions not to scale

625W P2/10 Clear
1000W K4 Frosted
1000W P2/7 Clear
1250W P2/12 Clear

500W K1 Frosted

2000W RSE/79
or CP/43
1000W RSE/19
650W RSE/26
500W RSE/18
2000W CP/53
1000W PAR 64
CP/60
CP/61
CP/62
1000W
CSI/CID
G22

Figure 15–1.   Lamp types. A selection of lamp types for concert lighting. (Courtesy Rank Strand.)

Profile spots can be adjusted for round size with an iris, shape with shutters, and beam edge with a lens (Figure 15–3). Adjusting the lens allows for a hard or soft edge. A smooth, even beam is the most suitable for most applications. The lenses should be mounted with the curved (convex) sides facing each other and the flat sides facing the outside and bulb. *Gobos* (metal stencils) can be placed in profile spots so that the image of the gobo is projected onto a screen or cyclorama.

Figure 15–2.   Par cans hold par 64 bulbs and raylight kits.

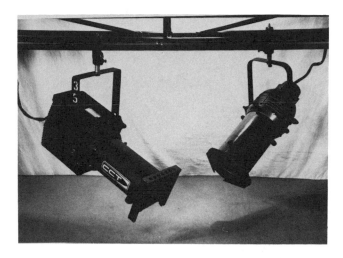

Figure 15–3. Profile spots. Their round size can be adjusted with an iris and shaped with shutters.

Fresnel spots let you adjust between a flood and a spot by means of moving the bulb behind the lens. Closer to the lens is a flood, and away from it is a spot.

The *ground row* provides four cells for four separate control channels and colors. Each cell supplies an even spread of light for lighting cycloramas or scenery.

Molefay lamps are internal reflector lamps that radiate a beam of intense light and heat. They are used in banks of eight for audience lighting and general flood.

High-intensity arc-type lights are used in follow spots and in some computerized lamps. These lamps require ballast to operate. To maintain optimum results, the quartz arc tube should not be handled. Operating the lamp for periods of less than 3 minutes seriously shortens the life of the lamp.

Most lamps work on the principle of heating a piece of wire, the filament, to the point at which it gives off light. Filaments are weakened when they are heated and are in their most delicate state while on or still warm. To avoid rough treatment of a lamp while it is on, approximate focusing of the lamps should be done at ground level so that only slight adjustment is needed in the air when the lamp is on.

With the development of microchip technology has come computerized lights (Figure 15–4). Varying degrees of technology are built around a light source. The most sophisticated models can alter pan, tilt, beam size, color, and beam shape and change with split-second timing through every degree

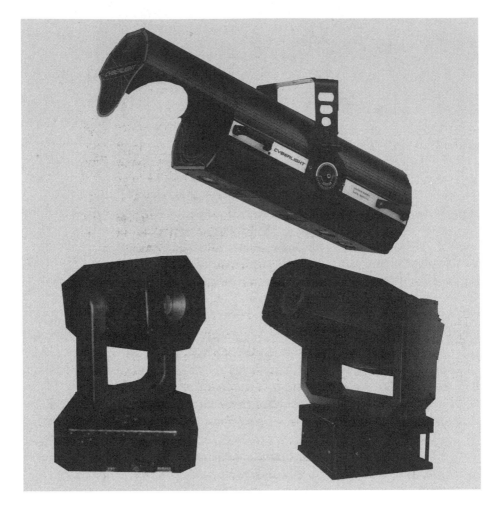

Figure 15–4.   Various types of automated instruments. VARI*LITE, Cyberlight, and Icon.

of color in the spectrum. The most unsophisticated instruments have limited color change, movement, and beam controls. Lamps used in conjunction with a sophisticated control console give a designer an infinite number of possibilities—the only limit is the imagination.

Color changers can be fitted to the front of most lamps to provide a scroll of color that is moved on rollers. The color changer is controlled by either a manual or a memory console.

HANGING LAMPS

Lamps generally are hung on the rails of trusses with hook clamps. Bars of lamps also have hook clamps. The lamps hung on the grid must have safety wires attached, gel-frame properly seated, and have undergone testing and rough focusing before the grid is raised. Anything that falls from the truss can cause serious injury. Tape any cables running along the trusses firmly in place so they do not hinder the crew.

Lamps often are situated on the floor as well as on the grid. These lights are likely to be moved, usually because of people's ignorance of lighting and the precise nature of focusing. Any cables run out to floor lamps should cross audio cables at right angles to avoid main-induced hum in the audio cables.

CHAPTER 16

DIMMERS

HOW A DIMMER WORKS

A *dimmer* is an electronic device that controls the amount of power used by a load. It turns off parts of the main waveform to reduce the amount of time the lamp receives main voltage. Switching on a variable portion of the main waveform controls the amount of power sent to a lamp. This is known as *phase control*. The devices that switch the main waveform are collectively known as *thyristors*. These are divided into two groups: *triacs* and *silicon-controlled rectifiers* (SCRs).

The thyristor is like a switch controlled by a trigger pulse. To provide control for SCR triggering, a voltage that falls at a set rate during the main half cycle is generated and resets to a maximum level when the main wave-form passes through the 0 V point. The voltage generated is called a *ramp* because of its shape.

Ramp voltage is compared with DC control voltage from the console (between 0 and 10 V), and an *oscillator-enable pulse* is generated whenever control voltage is greater than ramp voltage. The oscillator produces a stream of very narrow pulses for the duration of the oscillator-enable pulse and triggers the gate of the SCR, turning it on. The ramp voltage waveform generated in the dimmers is reset and repeated every main half cycle. The control voltage input is internally compared with ramp voltage, and the thyristors are triggered, when control voltage exceeds ramp voltage. Low control voltage triggers the thyristors late in the half cycle, giving low-output power. Higher control voltage triggers the thyristors earlier, giving higher-output power. The shape of the ramp voltage therefore governs the control law of the dimmer.

RAMPS

The *square law ramp,* established as a standard by the United States Illuminating Engineering Society, takes into account the nonlinear response of the human eye to changes in light intensity. For a control level of 50%, you would see a light level 50% of maximum.

A *true power ramp* gives an output of 50% for a setting of 50%. A 1,000 W bulb uses only 500 watts at a 50% setting. With an *exponential ramp*, light output varies the most in the control range of 70% to 100%. The *linear ramp* is not a curve but is a straight line with the greatest variation in light output at settings between 30% and 70%. The *luminance ramp* is similar to the square law ramp for settings above 40%. Below this level light output increases rapidly compared with a square law ramp. Finally, a *switching ramp* allows on-off control; below 50% the channel is off and above 50% it is on full.

TYPES OF DIMMERS

Dimmers are packaged in several different ways. Those packaged for touring should be able to remain patched for transportation (Figure 16–1). The size of a dimmer is measured in the amount of power it can handle. The most common sizes of dimmers for touring are 2.5 and 5 kW. A 2.5 kW dimmer can supply power to two 1,250 W bulbs or five 500 W bulbs. A 5 kW dimmer can supply 5,000 W of power. If the dimmer is presented with more power than it can handle, the fuse will blow. The types of connectors on dimmer packs and the voltage vary. Some dimmers are mounted in lamp bars, which assign a control channel on the bar.

DIMMER PATCHING

Patching is plugging the lamps into the dimmers with the correct control channel. The looms from the lamps terminate in different ways, but the principles are the same. Each lamp terminates at the rack as a single circuit. Take care that no 120 V lamps are patched into 240 V dimmers unless they are on a series splitter (twofer). A 120 V lamp cannot be paired with a 240 V lamp. If two lamps are paired in series, supposedly with 120 V bulbs, and one is bright and one is dull, the bulbs are mismatched. The dull one is the 240 V lamp and should be changed for a 120 V lamp. Aircraft lamps are 28 V, and four lamps in series constitute one 120 V circuit.

Figure 16–1.   Dimmer rack. Dimmers packaged for touring should be able to remain patched for transportation. (Courtesy Avolites.)

CHAPTER 17

CONTROL CABLES

The control cable carries the control voltage from the console to the dimmers. The console sends a voltage between 0 and 10 V DC depending on the console setting. Each console channel connects to the dimmer racks, where it is patched to the appropriate dimmers. Along with the console control cables are intercom lines and a power feed for the console.

Muliplex systems use digital information to control the dimmers. The console sends a string of digital data to each dimmer, which receives the information allocated to it. The digital multiplex code uses paired shielded cable rather than multicore cable, and a pair of wires is used for each control channel (Figure 17–1).

CARE OF MULTICORE CABLES

Before running the multiway cables to the console, check that there are no restrictions on the route you select (Figure 17–2). Cables usually must be strung up above fire exit doorways or run through a duct. The connectors should be protected with a padded sock and should never be dragged along the ground. If a connector snags, a great deal of soldering is needed.

A fault with the multicore cable can be easily found. Console output should be 1O V DC. Read the output connector on the console then the one on the end of the cable that connects to the dimmer racks. If there is no reading on the console connector, a console fault exists. A lighting system schematic is shown in Figure 17–3.

Figure 17–1.   Multiway connectors on a lighting board.

Figure 17–2.   Multiway cable. Before running the multiway cable to the console, make sure there are no restrictions on the route.

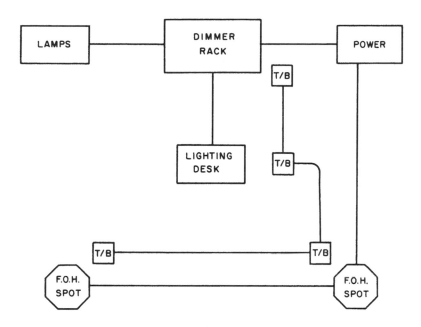

Figure 17–3.   Lighting system schematic. Connections between console, dimmers, and lamps.

CHAPTER 18

CONTROL CONSOLES

The control console is used to control the level of each channel and group channels together into scenes.

MANUAL CONSOLES

Manual consoles take the operator's physical movements of the faders and send a control voltage to the dimmers directly related to the position of the fader on the console (Figure 18–1). A fader position of five sends a 5 V DC signal to the dimmer to which it is connected. The more channels on a console, the more complex can scenes become. Most consoles have two presets, which allow the scenes to be preset and then faded in by the scene master.

Scene control masters are used to control the level of the scene patched into the pin matrix, which has a series of sockets that receive a pin (Figure 18–2). Each channel has a socket, and the number of scenes determines the number of times each channel is repeated. When the pins are inserted, each scene master brings up the channels that are pinned. Each channel has a flash button for instant full power, and the matrix masters also have flash buttons. Some consoles have chasers pinned on the matrix and have step control.

COMPUTER CONSOLES

Computer consoles have the same functions as manual consoles, but they have a large memory and can store several complex scenes (Figures 18–3 and

Figure 18–1. Manual console. The operator must move the faders to control the dimmers.

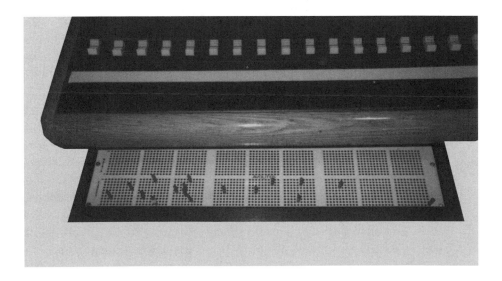

Figure 18–2. Pin matrix. Scenes are patched into the pin matrix with special pins.

Figure 18–3.   Computer consoles have a large memory and can remember several complex scenes.

18–4). The computer can record different levels for channels, unlike the matrix system, which has a fixed level. The chase sequences in a computer console are much more sophisticated than those on manual consoles.

Before attempting to operate a computer console, study the console manual. After you understand the book completely, begin to acquire hands-on experience. The most important thing about operating any console is the timing. All the computers in the world cannot make you a terrific lighting operator. Sensitive, accurate timing to create a mood and give a song more dramatic impact is the key to good operation.

Figure 18–4.   VARI*LITE Artisan control console. The console is the heart of the VARI*LITE Series 200 automated lighting system. (Courtesy Vari-Lite, Inc.)

CHAPTER 19

INTERCOM SYSTEMS

The intercom system allows the lighting crew to communicate during a show. The lighting director can cue follow spot operators, and the stage manager can call start and finish cues for the house light operator. Good communication is necessary for a smooth performance (Figure 19–1). Each headset is fitted with a microphone. The belt pack, which connects the headphones to the system, has a call button that lights when any station is calling, an on-off switch for the microphone, and a volume control for station level.

Keep the stations off metal objects such as spot stands. If the station finds a second earth reference, the system may hum, which makes extremely difficult to hear. The microphone should be switched off at all stations unless it is being used. Any microphones left on amplify any spill, which competes with the person speaking and makes it difficult to hear.

Stations must be distributed to all follow spot, dimmer, house light control, and console operators. A station is needed for the stage manager at the stage entrance for cueing the house light operators. Other stations may be needed for curtain cues, pyrotechnics, and so on.

Figure 19–1.   Intercom headphones and belt pack. The intercom system allows the lighting crew to communicate during a show.

CHAPTER 20

SMOKE MACHINES

Smoke is used to create many effects. The smoke provides a medium for the beams of light so that the beams can be seen rather than just illuminating the stage floor. All smoke machines become hot as part of the process of making the smoke and must be handled very carefully.

FOGGERS

Fog machines use water- or oil-based fluids to produce a vapor that looks like puffy smoke and is spread across the stage with fans. Because fluid vaporization is never complete, a residue eventually builds up and must be cleaned regularly to maintain optimum machine performance. Place the fog machine so that the area in front of it is clear enough for the vapor to dissipate.

DRY ICE MACHINES

The difference between dry ice and fog is that dry ice vapor falls to the floor whereas fog rises. Dry ice machines are like big kettles that heat water. The ice is lowered into the boiling water to produce vapor, which looks like smoke. Fans and flexible tubing are needed to move the vapor to where it is needed.

Dry ice burns the skin; wear gloves when handling it. The ice comes in blocks or pellets, and the blocks must be broken up so that the ice is evenly distributed in the machine. Do not let the machine boil dry. Turn the machine

123

off when it is not in use. Remember to allow time for the water to boil before the smoke effect is needed.

PYROTECHNICS

The term *pyrotechnics* refers to any flash or bang. Many stage fireworks are available. Because fireworks are dangerous, the operator must be licensed.

CRACKED OIL

Cracked-oil smoke is made by exposing a fine oil to compressed air. The air compressor is connected to outlet tanks that contain the oil. The compressed air is fed into the oil through a collection of spray jets. A fine mist results.

CHAPTER 21

DRAPES

All drapes must be fireproofed and are required by law to be labeled with the date and method of fire retardation. The drapes should have their size marked on them and on the center position. Be careful when handling drapes because they are very delicate. The drapes should be the last thing added to the grid before it is hoisted to its operating height. Keep the drapes tied up and out of the way until it is necessary to lower them for focusing once the stage has been set.

BLACK DRESSING

Black drapes are used to mask off stage hardware and form a boundary for the performing area. The drape at the rear of the stage is called a *backdrop*. The narrow strips of drape hung on either side of the stage to mask the wings are called *legs*. The drapes used to mask the trusses are abbreviated drops called *borders*.

CYCLORAMAS

Cycloramas (cycs), plain cloths that close off the back of the stage, are hung down to stage level and extended up and out to create an impression of great space. Lay out a roll of plastic or cloth on the stage to keep the cyc clean while it is being attached (you cannot have a great space with a handprint in the middle).

SCRIMS AND GAUZES

Scrim and *gauze* are synonyms for a finely woven, delicate fabric used to create a translucent effect.

SCREENS

Rear-projection screens are used to display images projected from behind the screen. These screens are fire retardant because of the plastic material used in their manufacture. The screen provides a wide viewing angle of the images projected. A white screen provides bright and even images of rear projections. A gray screen, the most widely used, is good for medium-level ambient light conditions when a bright projected image is desired. A black screen is excellent for high ambient light conditions, giving the image greater contrast and deep colors more intensity and richness.

CURTAIN TRACKS

Curtain tracks are used for curtains that open or close during a performance. Tracks are used for front-of-stage curtains. In a theater this curtain is called the *house curtain*. Until they are removed, these curtains obscure the stage from the audience. Drapes part in the center when they open; opening drapes requires a smooth, consistent motion. Tracks may be used to display a range of backdrops, from black to white to painted. When sections of track are joined together, check them to make sure there will be no snags along the length of the track. It is a disaster when a curtain does not open when it should.

KABUKI DROPS

A kabuki drop is a method of removing a drape. The kabuki pipe from which the drape is suspended has a series of spikes onto which the drape is hooked. The pipe is fixed to a swivel mechanism. When the mechanism is rotated so that the spikes face downward, the drape falls to the floor with an even motion.

CHAPTER 22

FOLLOW SPOTS

Follow spots are used to light the focal points on the stage (Figure 22–1). The follow spots are operated manually; the operator controls the intensity, color, and movement of the spot. Follow spots are positioned in front of the stage in the venue or on the grid above the stage (Figure 22–2). The position of follow spots should be high so that the beam does not wash the entire stage and does not shine in the performer's eyes (Figure 22–3).

OPERATING FOLLOW SPOTS

A follow spot operator receives cues from the lighting director through the headphone intercom system. The follow spot operator should not switch off the microphone on the intercom station and should not speak to the director unless absolutely necessary. Spot cues usually are given as standby spot number, gel-frame number, and position. The command to change to the cue is always given with "go" as the last word. Cues may be given to follow certain action on the stage. It is important to give spotlight operators clear and distinct cues. Because the follow spots highlight the subject being spotted, any mistake is immediately obvious to the entire audience, the performers, and the crew.

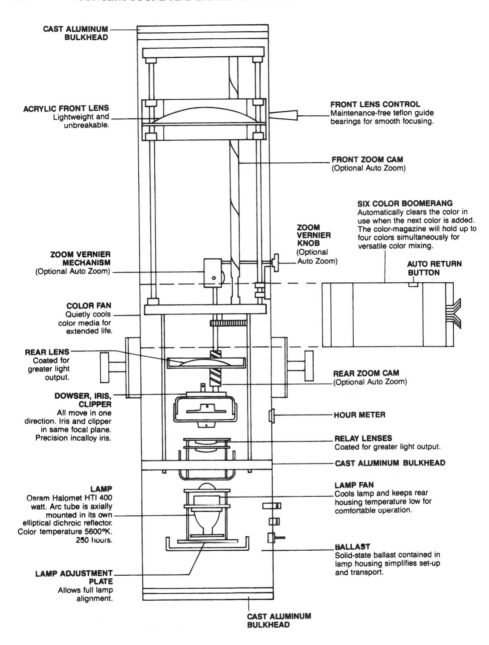

CAST ALUMINUM BULKHEAD

ACRYLIC FRONT LENS
Lightweight and unbreakable.

FRONT LENS CONTROL
Maintenance-free teflon guide bearings for smooth focusing.

FRONT ZOOM CAM
(Optional Auto Zoom)

SIX COLOR BOOMERANG
Automatically clears the color in use when the next color is added. The color-magazine will hold up to four colors simultaneously for versatile color mixing.

ZOOM VERNIER KNOB
(Optional Auto Zoom)

AUTO RETURN BUTTON

ZOOM VERNIER MECHANISM
(Optional Auto Zoom)

COLOR FAN
Quietly cools color media for extended life.

REAR LENS
Coated for greater light output.

REAR ZOOM CAM
(Optional Auto Zoom)

DOWSER, IRIS, CLIPPER
All move in one direction. Iris and clipper in same focal plane. Precision incalloy iris.

HOUR METER

RELAY LENSES
Coated for greater light output.

CAST ALUMINUM BULKHEAD

LAMP
Osram Halomet HTI 400 watt. Arc tube is axially mounted in its own elliptical dichroic reflector. Color temperature 5600°K. 250 hours.

LAMP FAN
Cools lamp and keeps rear housing temperature low for comfortable operation.

LAMP ADJUSTMENT PLATE
Allows full lamp alignment.

BALLAST
Solid-state ballast contained in lamp housing simplifies set-up and transport.

CAST ALUMINUM BULKHEAD

Figure 22–1. Ultra-arc follow spot. Follow spots are used to light the focal points of the stage. (Courtesy Phoebus Manufacturing.)

Figure 22–2.   Short-throw follow spot. These spots usually are positioned in the grid above the stage.

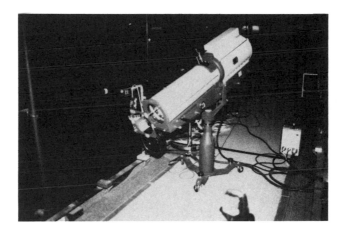

Figure 22–3.   Front of house follow spot. The position of follow spots should be high so the beam does not wash the stage or get into the performer's eyes.

CHAPTER 23

COLOR

Color gives the lighting designer a palette from which to work to create the moods and scenes that enhance a performance. The color media guide (Appendix A) outlines some recommendations for the use of the complete range of colors available. The recommendations are not hard and fast rules. Stage lighting is an art, not a science.

Some countries have stringent fire regulations prohibiting the use of certain gels. Self-extinguishing polycarbonate filters, such as Supergel by Rosco, comply with the most stringent requirements. All gels melt if there is any dust on the surface. The dust particles become like red-hot rocks with heat from the lamp.

Blue filters always fade more quickly than other colors. All filters change the color of the lamp by allowing part of the spectrum to pass through while absorbing all other colors. Blue absorbs green and red; red is in the hot pan of the spectrum. Heat makes the color evaporate, resulting in a faded filter.

Whenever any gel is cut, mark the color number on each piece with a grease pencil. The mark should be in the center of the filter so that it can be easily identified from the ground.

Patterns or gobos are metal stencils placed in profile spots to project the stenciled image. A number of composite patterns can be used to create animated effects (Figure 23–1). Mesh is used to shade certain patterns. A wide range of gobos are available to give special effects without special equipment, and they can be used boldly or subtly to good effect.

Figure 23–1. Composite pattern. A number of composite patterns can be used to create animated patterns. (Courtesy Rosco Laboratories.)

CHAPTER 24

LIGHTING PLOTS

Most of the information that relates to a lighting system is contained on the plot. Lamp types, position, control channel, gel color, and cable numbers are marked on the plot. Because the plot is the point of reference for any lighting system, it is necessary to know how to read the plot and put together the equipment to turn the plot into a working system (Figure 24–1).

READING A LIGHTING PLOT

Draw the lighting plot to scale to allow calculation of the number of truss sections, corners, truss rigging, chain motors, lamp positioning, and length of cables required. The legend, or means of notation, can be presented in different ways, so always check the legend of each plot. The legend allows you to calculate the number and type of lamps, number of cables, number of dimmers, power requirements, and number of control channels. The position and size of drapes, whether truss borders, legs, cycloramas, or backdrops, should be marked on the plot.

Several lists can be drawn up from the plot to order the correct equipment. Many plots supply additional information to clarify trim heights, follow spot requirements, smoke or pyrotechnic effects, number of talkback stations, dimmer position, and control console position. A system list itemizes types of lamps, number and lengths of cables, accessories and dressing, rigging, and trussing (Figures 24–2 through 24–4).

A gel-color-filter cutting list can be drawn up so that the right amount of gel is cut to fit the lamps being used.

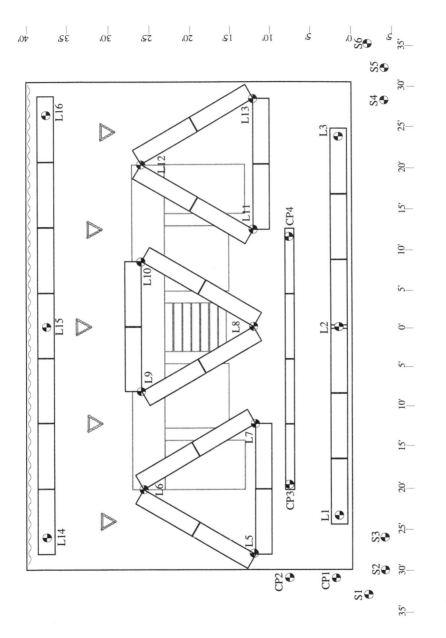

Figure 24–1. Rigging plot. Draw the plot to scale to allow calculation of trusses and motor positions. (Courtesy of Sean Hackett.)

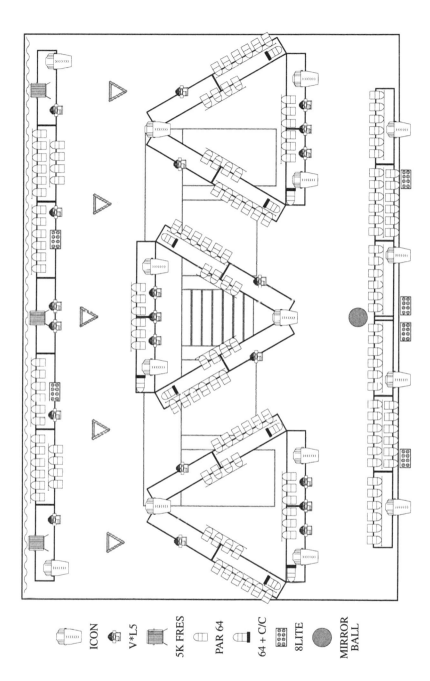

Figure 24–2. Lighting plot. Lamp types, position, control channel, gel color, and cable numbers are marked on the plot. (Courtesy of Sean Hackett.)

ICON

V*L5

5K FRES

PAR 64

64 + C/C

8LITE

MIRROR BALL

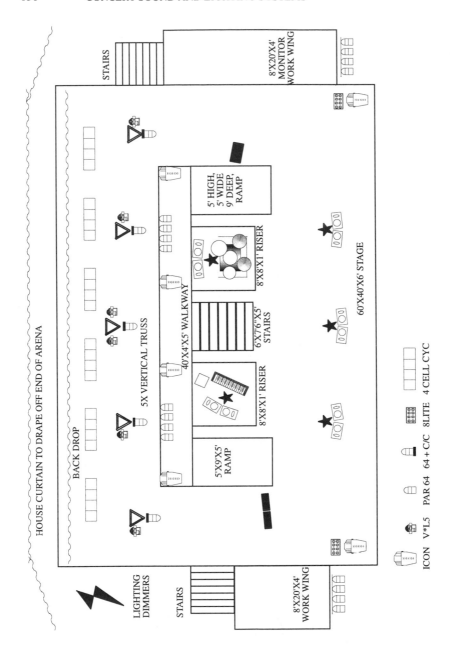

Figure 24–3.   Stage plan and lighting layout. (Courtesy of Sean Hackett.)

Figure 24-4.   Set plan with two-dimensional perspective. (Courtesy of Sean Hackett.)

CIRCUIT CODING

The dimmer patch must be worked out to identify the control channel and lamps connected to each of the dimmers. The lamps are identified according to the code of the cable that connects the lamp to the dimmers. The circuit code identifies the position of the lamps on the grid. In some circumstances the position of a lamp does not lend itself to standard coding, necessitating special circuit codes. A standard code can be used for identifying the circuits of a lighting system.

Coding of cross-stage trusses starts at the front downstage rail of the bar of lamps nearest to the dimmers, beginning with A1. Subsequent bars or circuits are coded A2, A3, and so on. Once the downstage rail is coded, the upstage rail of the front truss is coded B1, B2, and so on. The letters I and 0 are not used to avoid confusion with one and zero. The lowest number always is on the dimmer side of the stage.

All trusses running upstage and downstage use DSL for downstage left, USL for upstage left, DSR for downstage right, and USR for upstage right. Lamps hung in a vertical array use L1, L2, and so on for stage left and R1, R2, and soon for stage right. Lamps positioned diagonally are marked XL for cross-stage left and XR for cross-stage right.

Any lamps positioned on the stage and not on the grid are identified with the code FL followed by a number. Ground rows and cyclorama lights are coded GR followed by a number, the lowest number being closest to the dimmers.

PUTTING TOGETHER A SYSTEM

Once all the lists have been drawn up from the information on the plot, the system can be assembled. Use copies of the plot as a checklist to mark off the items prepared, checked, coded, and packed. A system that has been well prepared and coded can be assembled quickly at the venue (Figure 24–5).

All lamp bars can be gelled and the correct bulb type fitted and marked with the circuit code. The bars must be checked for loose or stripped screws or loose or frayed cables and repaired as needed. It is far easier to repair items on the ground than to try to fix them while they are 20 feet in the air.

The cables that carry the power to the lamps can be strapped together and coded. All the cables distributing the circuits to a truss can be loomed, but the number of cables strapped together should remain manageable. It is pointless to have an unmanageable loom that becomes a tangled mess. Any adapters necessary to convert the end of a multiway cable to individual circuits can be attached and marked. Individual circuits are required for lamps not on bars.

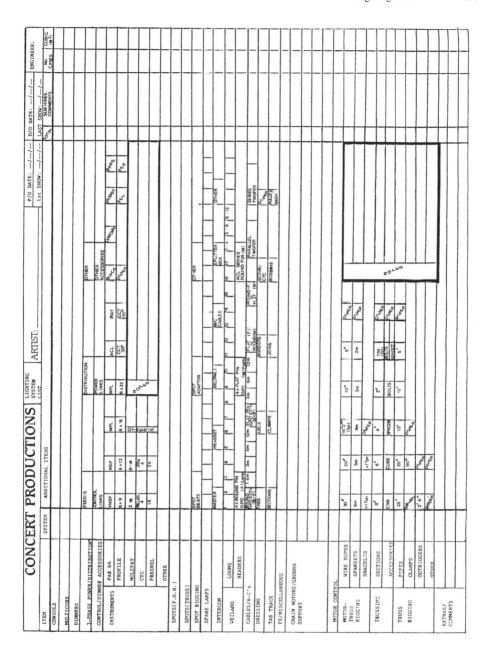

Figure 24–5.   Lighting system list. A well-prepared and coded system can be assembled quickly at the venue.

Ellipsoidal spots must have the lenses and reflectors cleaned and the mechanical parts checked for smooth operation. Any gobos can be fitted. These lamps can accept a variety of bulbs with different voltages and wattages as long as they are clearly marked; a 120 V bulb lasts a fraction of a second in a 240 V dimmer.

Check dimmers for any loose screws or electrical faults. Dimmers should be patched and marked clearly with the circuit code so that all the cables can be automatically plugged into the correct sockets. Patching the dimmers requires a great deal of concentration. The best time to patch them is when there is peace and quiet, which is not during setup. The dimmers not only provide the circuitry to control the amount of power sent to each lamp but also distribute power to all the lamps. The power distribution system must therefore be checked for any burnt connectors and loose wires. Dealing with a large number of instruments requires a great deal of power. Any mistakes or faults can be extremely dangerous and costly.

Check whatever is being used to fasten the truss sections together. The correct number of snap-out pipes, 90-degree scaffold clamps, swivel clamps, and pipes must be packed. Clamps should be checked for any stripped or jammed threads.

Drapes should be checked for ties and runners and to ensure that they have no tears and are clean. Mark the size of the drape on each corner and make a center mark. All drapes used for shows must be fireproof and marked with the fireproofing method and date. All curtain tracks must be checked for bends and snags.

Cut and install the gels for the follow spots. All follow spots must be checked for mechanical and electrical function and have clean lenses. Spots to be positioned on the truss need the correct hardware for mounting and seats with seat belts for the operators.

Smoke machines deteriorate quickly if not maintained. They must be cleaned regularly to remove any blockages that inhibit the flow of smoke. The amount of fog fluid depends on the number of performances.

Label the control console and check the functions and multicore cables. It often is not possible to assemble an entire lighting system before it is set up at a venue because of the amount of space and power necessary, which makes checking the console functions difficult. Do any programming or matrix patching that you can before setup.

The power feeder cable that brings power from the supply to the distribution board for the dimmer racks must be able to connect to the supply. The connection is either through screw terminals or bolted onto a bar with lugs. If in doubt, make sure you have the correct lugs for the cable.

The intercom system used for cueing spotlight operators must be in perfect condition, since coordination of the show relies on it. Spare headsets and belt packs should always be available.

Chain motors and rigging equipment have stringent safety laws. Do not use any piece of rigging equipment you suspect is faulty. The motor control and motors must be checked electrically and physically. Enough slings and shackles should be packed to enable the motors to be rigged where required and allow for height and bridles.

Work lights, tools, ladders, gaffer tape, insulating tape, and spare lamps, clamps, bolts, and fuses are needed. All cases that have been packed should have their estimated weights marked on them.

Now that various pieces of lighting equipment have been packed as a lighting system, gelled up, and coded for a particular show, the boxes can be loaded into the truck and taken to the venue. Remember that heavy boxes go on the bottom and light ones on the top. Keep same-sized cases in blocks as much as possible. Work out a truck pack before the truck is loaded; rigging cases and motors should be the first cases unloaded, so load them last. Pack the cases in tightly and strap them to reduce damaging vibration.

CHAPTER 25

LIGHTING SYSTEM SETUP PROCEDURE

SETUP

The setup procedure outlines the series of events that result in the lighting system's being ready for a show. Each design requires its own specialized approach because the number of lamps always varies, as do positions and the amount of time available to set up. The order of events is the same whatever the size of the rig and the number of crew setting up. The larger a system is, the more things are done by more crew simultaneously. Keep copies of the lighting plot on hand so that everyone can refer to them. The pressure usually is on the lighting crew to get the lighting grid in the air as quickly as possible so that the stage can be set with sound and band equipment. It is important to communicate with the other members of the production crew so that setup can be a coordinated procedure.

Unloading the Truck

One member of the lighting crew should stay in the truck as it is being unloaded to ensure that the equipment is handled properly and nothing is dropped or damaged (Figure 25–1). Other crew members should stay in the venue and direct and assist the equipment to the desired locations as it is

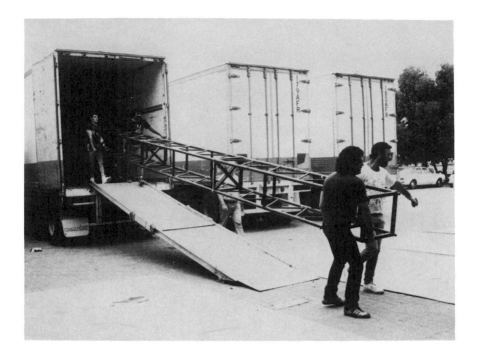

Figure 25–1.   Unloading the truck. One lighting crew member should stay in the truck to ensure stagehands unload everything properly.

brought in. All cases should be clearly marked for desired location so that minimum direction is required. The color code is as follows:

Red: Stage left
Yellow: Stage right
Green: Front of house (FOH)
Orange: On stage

Rigging

Chalk the position of the points required on the stage so the riggers can see them from the ceiling. The chain motors must be positioned and any rigging necessary attached to the motor hook.

The chain motor power must be connected and the phasing checked so that the motor moves in the intended direction (Figure 25–2). Motor control cables can be run along the trusses to the motor controller, so that as soon as each motor is rigged, it can be lifted and attached to the truss. As soon as the last motor is rigged, the grid should be ready to be lifted. When the trusses

Figure 25–2.   Rigging a chain motor. Chain motor power must be checked for correct phasing so that the motor moves in the direction intended.

are supported on ground supports, the ground should be solid and level. If a ground support is not leveled, it leans, the truss is hoisted higher, and the risk for an accident increases.

Power Connection

The three-phase connection usually is made by the venue electrician or a qualified outside electrician. Establish the location and rating of the fuses or breakers in the event of a power failure. The power connection should begin as soon as the cable is unloaded. The cable should be one of the first things off the truck because the venue electrician may not be used to working at the same pace as a touring crew.

Assembling the Trusses

As the truss sections arrive on stage, they must be positioned and connected. Each connection must be checked at each setup (Figure 25–3). While the grid is being assembled, all additional pipes and outriggers can be fitted, borders attached, and truss spots mounted.

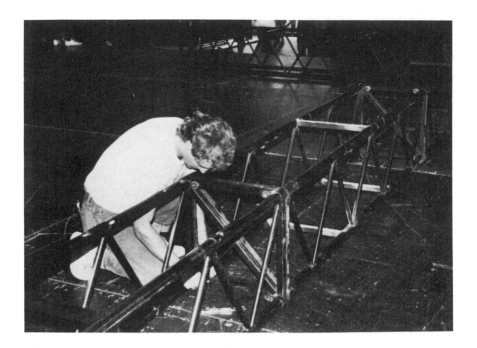

Figure 25–3.   Assembling the trusses. Each connection must be checked at each setup.

Looming

While the points are being rigged, which can sometimes take longer than desired, the looms can be run out and attached to the trusses.

Hanging the Lamps

As soon as the grid is lifted, it is time to hang the lamps. The bars of lamps should be marked with their coded number, the same number on the cable that connects the bar to the dimmers. Mark the position of each bar on the trusses; if this is not possible, check the position of the lamps. Once the cables are connected, the looms can be tested to reveal any faults. Check the lamps to make sure the gel frame is seated safely, all bolts are secure, and the gel is in good condition. Do a rough focus now so that minimal adjustment is necessary later. Lamps sometimes are damaged in transit or just bum out, so make sure they all work before the grid is raised to its operating height. It is much easier to change lamps with your feet firmly on the ground (Figure 25–4).

Drapes

While the lamps are being checked, all the drapes can be attached to the grid. Check legs and borders for neatness and symmetry and tab tracks for any

Figure 25–4.   Hanging lamps. Do a rough focus so that minimal adjustment is necessary during formal focusing.

snags. The legs and backdrop may have to be tied until later in setup so that they do not restrict access onto the stage.

Raising the Grid

When the lamps, looms, and drapes are ready, attach the ladder, drop bag, and trim chains. While the grid is being raised, the person operating the chain hoists must ensure that no one is standing under it (Figure 25–5). Once the grid is at its operating height, each point must be trimmed to its exact height as measured with the trim chains. Raise cable picks with the grid to reduce the weight of the looms on the grid. When trusses are being lifted on ground supports, raise them evenly so that one support does not become overloaded.

Dimmers

Now that the grid is up at trim and the stage is clear, the dimmers can be patched. By this time the electrician should have connected the power, which can be checked before it is connected to the power distribution for the dimmers. Set the console and run out the multicore control cable. Do a circuit check to find any dimmer faults (Figure 25–6).

Figure 25–5.   Raising the grid. When the grid is being raised, the person operating the chain hoists must ensure that no one is standing under it.

Figure 25–6.   Dimmers. The dimmer racks assign the correct control channel to each lamp.

Follow Spots

If follow spots must be hoisted onto catwalks or cradles, the riggers should sling the spots so that they are not dropped. Once they are in position, the spots can be set up and focused. While the spots are being set, the intercom can be run out and checked. The intercom must run to all spots, dimmers, console, house light control, and stage entrance.

Floor Lamps

After the stage has been set with sound and band equipment, position the floor lamps, smoke machines, and fans. Cables that run across the stage should be kept as far away as possible from audio cables. Lighting cables should cross audio cables at right angles if necessary and not run parallel to them.

Focus

The easiest way to focus is while it is quiet. It is best if focusing can be coordinated with piano tuning or the sound crew's break. The more lamps to focus, the more organized you must be. The lighting director should know exactly where each lamp on the plot is to be focused. The stage can be marked with the spacing for lamps so that symmetrical beams are focused accurately. A list of channels for the focus can be given to the board operator so that the lighting director can stay on stage and direct focusing. A hand signal or whistle tells the board operator to move to the next channel. Use of an intercom station on stage during focusing obviates screaming. It is dangerous to climb on trusses in the dark, so concentration is necessary.

SHOW TIME

During the show the lighting crew may be involved with operating the console, operating a follow spot, operating smoke machines, opening and closing curtains, or watching the dimmers. The start and finish of the show should be coordinated with the stage manager so that the house lights go off and come on when they are supposed to.

LOAD OUT

Get the floor lamps off the stage and the console, multicore cables, and dimmers packed while the stage is being cleared. Once the stage is cleared, the grid can be lowered and the rig dismantled, cased, and loaded onto the truck.

MAINTENANCE

Daily maintenance is required because the electrical equipment and lamps are fragile. Wheels are smashed, cables are damaged, and lamps are broken, so regular maintenance is a good idea.

SAFETY

Safety in rigging, both mechanical and electrical, cannot be overemphasized. Time is always short because show time is always looming, and it may seem tempting to cut corners and in the process miss a loose nut or frayed cable. The only way to avoid accidents is to check, check again, and keep checking. For example, do not block fire exits, fire extinguishers, or hoses with empty cases. Do not leave cables under load coiled up; they can melt and possibly cause a fire. Keep an electrical fire extinguisher next to the dimmers. Some cities have very strict regulations about dimmer positions and require that dimmers be set in mesh cages. Safety chains or wires are necessary for all lamps suspended above the stage (Figure 25–7). Finally, before climbing the ladder onto the grid or trusses, empty your pockets of coins and tools!

Figure 25–7.   Safety wire on lamps. Safety chains or wires are necessary for all lamps suspended above stage.

COLOR MEDIA GUIDE: SUGGESTIONS ON HOW TO USE SUPERGEL AND ROSCOLENE COLOR FILTERS

ACTING AREAS/WARM

The color range here includes amber, pink, straw, and salmon, with several choices in each color category. These colors are often cross lit with those recommended for cool acting areas. The warm colors suggest daylight and brightness. They are generally used for scenes set in the morning or noon.

Supergel		Roscolene		Applications
01	Light Bastard Amber	802	Bastard Amber	Enhances fair skin tones. Suggests strong sunlight.
		803	Pale Gold	Good where a tint of color is needed. Excellent for natural skin tones.
03	Dark Bastard Amber			Most saturated Bastard Amber.
04	Medium Bastard Amber			Especially useful when cross lit with a cool color. Excellent for natural sunlight.
05	Rose Tint			Excellent area light and warm cosmetic color.
06	No Color Straw	804	No Color Straw	Slightly off-white. Good for interiors.
07	Pale Yellow			Double saturation of 06.
		805	Light Straw	Less green than 07. Excellent realistic sunlight in a light-colored show.
		808	Medium Straw	Warmer straw. Flattering to skin tones. Useful for dance.
09	Pale Amber Gold			Deep straw. Late afternoon sunsets.
30	Light Salmon Pink			Excellent for general area washes. Gives overall warming effect to skin tones.
31	Salmon Pink	834	Salmon Pink	General wash. Good for follow spots. Useful in a warm and cool combination.
		835	Medium Salmon Pink	Similar uses as 31 and 834. Provides deeper tones.
33	No Color Pink	825	No Color Pink	A pale, almost colorless pink. A popular color among dance-lighting designers.
		826	Flesh Pink	Useful for bright musicals.

Supergel	Roscolene	Applications
35A Light Pink		Close to 33.
36A Medium Pink		Good for general washes and cross lighting.
38 Light Rose		Greater saturation with uses similar to those of 36A.

ACTING AREAS/COOL

Blue and violet are the colors on the cool side of the spectrum. There are probably more shades of blue than of any other color represented in Supergel and Roscolene because virtually every stage production requires some blue in the palette.

Supergel	Roscolene	Applications
61 Mist Blue (greener)		Excellent for general area washes. Very light cool tint of blue. Helps maintain white light when dimmer is at low intensity.
63 Pale Blue (greener)		
64 64 Light Steel Blue		Useful beams of realistic moonlight.
65 Daylight Blue		Useful for achieving depressed moods and dull skies.
66	848 Water Blue	Good cold light. Pale greenish blue, useful moonlight source.
	849 Pale Blue (greener)	
67 Light Sky Blue	851 Daylight Blue	Excellent sky color. Useful for eye and border lights.
	852 Smoky Blue (redder)	
70 Nile Blue	850 No Color Blue	Useful for very light midday skies.
71 Sea Blue	853 Middle Blue (greener)	Occasionally used for general cool tint.
72 Azure Blue		

ACTING AREAS/NEUTRAL

These colors, in the lavender, gray, and blue ranges, work as complementary colors for both the warm and cool area colors or where just a touch of color is desirable. The Supergel diffusers offer the designer extra flexibility.

Supergel	*Roscolene*	*Applications*
	840 Surprise Lavender	Touch of color when white light is not desirable. Good on costumes or when instruments are down on dimmer.
52 Light Lavender		Excellent for general area or border light washes. It is a basic follow spot color.
53 Pale Lavender		Use when a touch of color is needed. Use when white light is not desirable.
54 Special Lavender		Same as 53.
55 Lilac (bluer)		Same as 53.
57A Lavender	841 Surprise Pink (redder)	Gives good visibility without destroying night illusions.
58A Deep Lavender	842 Special Lavender	Excellent backlight. Enhances dimensionality.
	844 Violet	
78 Trudy Blue		Rich medium blue.
	880 Light Gray	Usually used in combination with light tints of color.
	853 Medium Gray (very dark)	Reduces the brightness of color but does not affect hue on saturation. Useful where dimmer control or lower wattage lamp is not practical.
	882 Light Chocolate	Warms light and reduces intensity.
100 Frost	801 Frost	
101 Light Frost		
104 Tough Silk		
113 Matte Silk		
114 Hamburg Frost		
120 Red Diffusion		

Supergel	Roscolene	Applications
121 Blue Diffusion		
122 Green Diffusion		
123 Amber Diffusion		

Note: Numbers 100, 101, 104, 113, 114, 120, 121, 122, and 123 are effects colors that are used with color to create different dispersion characteristics.

ACCENTS/WARM

These colors, which embrace a wide range of yellow, amber, pink, orange, and magenta, are frequently used in sidelights, downlights, and backlights. They add a warm cast while sculpting actors, scenery, or props with light.

Supergel	Roscolene	Applications
10 Medium Yellow		Yellow with green. Good for special effects. Accent unflattering in acting areas.
11 Light Straw		Pale yellow with slight red content. Useful for candle effects. Can be used for area lighting and for bright day feeling.
	806 Medium Lemon	Less green than 10. Unflattering in acting areas. Useful for contrast lighting, accents, hot-day sunlight.
	807 Dark Lemon	Darker than 806 with a higher red content.
14 Medium Straw		Pale amber; higher red content than 12. Sunlight, accents, area lighting with caution to skin tones.
15 Deep Straw	809 Straw	Warm golden amber with some green. Useful for special effects such as candlelight and firelight. Tends to depress color pigment values. Use with care.
	810 No Color Amber	Good warm glow color for fire effect.

Supergel	Roscolene	Applications
	811 Flame	Warm pinkish amber. Afternoon sunset. Good sidelight.
	813 Light Amber	Dark pink amber. Sunlight. Deep sunsets.
20 Medium Amber		Afternoon sunlight, lamplight, and candlelight. Tends to depress color pigment values.
	815 Golden Amber	Greater red content than 20. Useful for torchlight and light from wood fires. Use with great care. Destroys most pigment color values.
21 Golden Amber	817 Dark Amber	Useful as amber eye light and late sunsets.
23 Orange		Provides a romantic sunlight through windows for evening effects.
32 Medium Salmon Pink		Deepest of the salmon pinks.
40 Light Salmon		Similar to 23 with a higher red content.
	827 Bright Pink	Basic follow spot color. Useful for live entertainment and as strong accent.
	829 Bright Rose	Less saturation than 827.
	830 Medium Pink	Use in romantic settings. Often used in dance.
	828 Follies Pink	Musical pink. Lush accents. Very versatile color.
48 Rose Purple		Pale evening color. Excellent for backlight.
	838 Dark Magenta	Greater intensity than 48.
	839 Rose Purple	Greater intensity than 838.
49 Medium Purple		Darkest of the magenta purple range.
50A Mauve	836 Plush Pink	Subdued sunlight effect. Useful in backlights.

ACCENTS/COOL

These shades of blue and green are widely used in evening or moonlight scenes in which additional color accents are needed. Like the warm accent colors, they are most frequently used in sidelights, downlights, and back-lights.

Supergel	Roscolene	Applications
65 Sky Blue		Excellent for early morning sky tones. Popular among designers for cycs and borders.
69 Brilliant Blue	856 Light Blue	Used for dramatic moonlight effects.
73 Peacock Blue	854 Steel Blue	Good for fantasy, moonlight, and water effects.
	855 Azure Blue Moonlight.	Natural sky on eye. Slightly greenish.
76 Light Green Blue	858 Light Green Blue	
77 Green Blue	859 Green Blue (Moonlight) (redder)	Distinctive greenish blues.
	860 Bright Blue	Useful for romantic moonlight.
	862 True Blue	
	861 Surprise Blue	Primary blue. For use with three-color light primary system in eye lighting.
	857 Light Medium Blue	
81 Urban Blue		Very cold brittle feeling.
52 Surprise Blue		Deep rich blue with slight amount of red.
86 Pea Green	878 Yellow Green	Good for dense foliage and woodland effects.
89 Moss Green	871 Light Green	Useful for mood, mystery, and toning.

CYC/SKY

The colors chosen for this group are often used for other purposes, but the shades of amber, red, blue, and green work particularly well on cycloramas. Cycs generally are used to set the horizon of the scene. On some stages blue-colored material is used for cycs, and these should be lit only with blue or green filters.

Supergel	Roscolene	Applications
	815 Golden Amber	Useful for torchlight and light from wood fires. Use with great care. Destroys most pigment color values.
21 Golden Amber	817 Dark Amber	Useful as amber eye light and late sunsets.
22 Deep Amber		Very useful as a backlight. Dramatic specials.
26 Light Red		Vibrant red. Good alternative primary.
	821 Light Red	Bright red. Alternative to primary red when higher light transmission is required.
27 Medium Red	823 Medium Red	Good red primary for use with three-color light primary systems in cyclorama lighting, footlights, and border lights.
	846 Medium Purple	Midnight and moonlight illusions. Enforces mysterious mood. Useful for evening cyc wash.
	843 Medium Lavender	Excellent for nighttime scenes Rich, vivid accents. Good in backgrounds. Unrealistic.
65 Daylight Blue		Useful for achieving depressed moods and dull skies.
67 Light Sky Blue	851 Daylight Blue	Excellent sky color.Useful for cyc and border.

Supergel	*Roscolene*	*Applications*
	852 Smoky Blue (redder)	
68 Sky Blue		Excellent for early morning sky tones. Popular among designers for cyc and borders.
69 Brilliant Blue	856 Light Blue	Used for dramatic moonlight effects.
73 Peacock Blue	854 Steel Blue	Good for fantasy, moonlight, and water effects.
	855 Azure Blue	Moonlight. Natural sky on cyc. Slightly greenish.
76 Light Green Blue	858 Light Green Blue	Distinctive greenish blues. Useful for romantic moonlight.
	859 Green Blue	Moonlight.
	860 Bright Blue (greener)	
	862 True Blue (bluer)	
	857 Light Medium Blue	Primary blue.
	861 Surprise Blue	For use with three-color light primary system in cyc lighting.
51 Urban Blue		Very cold, hard, brittle feeling.
82 Surprise Blue		Deep rich blue with slight amount of red.
	863 Dark Medium Blue (greener)	Good for nonrealistic night skies.
90 Dark Yellow Green	874 Medium Green	Alternative primary when higher transmission is desired.
95 Medium Blue Green	877 Medium Blue Green	Used on foliage in moonlight areas or for creating a mood of mystery. Good for toning scenery painted in blues, blue-greens, and greens.

SUNLIGHT

Some of these colors are repetitions of those listed under Acting Areas/Warm, but this group is limited to colors that most nearly approximate sunlight. Real sunlight changes color slightly as the day wears on, so colors should be chosen and color changes specified to coincide with the time of day.

Supergel	Roscolene	Applications
01 Light Bastard Amber	802 Bastard Amber	Enhances fair skin tones. Suggests strong sunlight.
04 Medium Bastard Amber		Especially useful when cross lit with a cool color. Excellent for natural sunlight.
	805 Light Straw	Less green than 07. Excellent realistic sunlight in a light-colored show.
09 Pale Amber Gold		Deep straw. Late afternoon sunsets.
10 Medium Yellow		Yellow with green. Good for special effects. Unflattering in acting areas.
11 Light Straw		Pale yellow with slight red content. Useful for candle effects. Can be used for area lighting and for bright day feeling.
	806 Medium Lemon	Less green than 10. Unflattering in acting areas. Useful for contrast-lighting accents and hot-day sunlight.
	807 Dark Lemon	Darker than 806 with a higher red content.

Supergel	Roscolene	Applications
14 Medium Straw		Pale amber; higher red content than 12. Sunlight, accents area lighting with caution to skin tones.
15 Deep Straw	809 Straw	Warm golden amber with some green. Useful for special effects. Candlelight and firelight tend to depress color pigment values. Use with care.
	810 No Color Amber	Good warm-glow color for fire effect.
	813 Light Amber	Dark pink amber. Sunlight. Deep sunsets.
20 Medium Amber		Afternoon sunlight, lamplight, and candlelight. Tends to depress color pigment values.
	815 Golden Amber	Greater red content than 20. Useful for torchlight and light from wood fires. Use with great care. Destroys most pigment color values.
	819 Orange Amber	Provides excellent effect in par fixtures.
25 Orange Red	818 Orange	Same as 819. Less red.
23 Orange		Provides romantic sunlight through windows for evening effects.
	869 Pale Yellow Green	Excellent accent tint. Soft tone frontlight at low dimmer readings.

MOONLIGHT

Moonlight is represented by lavender or blue, but there is a wide range of mood among the choices available. The shade of moonlight chosen usually reflects the mood of the play's action.

Supergel	Roscolene	Applications
57 Lavender	841 Surprise Pink (redder)	Excellent backlight. Gives good visibility without destroying night illusions.
58 Deep Lavender	842 Special Lavender	Enhances dimensionality.
	844 Violet	
65 Daylight Blue		Useful for achieving depressed moods and dull skies.
67 Light Sky Blue	851 Daylight Blue	Excellent sky color. Useful for eye and border.
	852 Smokey Blue (redder)	
68 Sky Blue		Excellent for early morning sky tones. Popular among designers for eye and borders.
69 Brilliant Blue	856 Light Blue	Used for dramatic moonlight effects.
	848 Water Blue	Pale greenish blue.
	849 Pale Blue (greener)	
70 Nile Blue	850 No Color Blue	Useful for very light midday skies. Occasionally used for general cool tint.
71 Sea Blue	853 Middle Blue (greener)	
72 Azure Blue		
73 Peacock Blue	854 Steel Blue	Good for fantasy, moonlight, and water effects.
	855 Azure Blue	Natural sky on cyc. Slightly greenish.
81 Urban Blue		Very cold, brittle feeling.
82 Surprise Blue		Deep, rich blue with slight amount of red.

NIGHT/EVENING

These shades of blue are used for night where moonlight may or may not be the basic form of illumination. Night is black, which is the absence of color. These colors allow the audience to see the action while maintaining the feeling of night.

Supergel	Roscolene	Applications
76 Light Green Blue	858 Light Green Blue	
	860 Bright Blue (greener)	Useful for romantic moonlight.
	862 True Blue (bluer)	
	861 Surprise Blue	Primary blue. For use with three-color light primary system in eye lighting.
	857 Light Medium Blue	
85 Deep Blue		

SPECIAL EFFECTS

This large group of colors may be used for special effects such as fire and ghosts, but special effects include special color accents that add just the right note to a stage picture. The descriptions should help locate the exact color needed. This group is above all others subject to imagination and style.

Supergel	Roscolene	Applications
10 Medium Yellow		Yellow with green. Good for special effects. Accent unflattering in acting areas.
11 Light Straw		Pale yellow with slight red content. Useful for candle effects. Can be used for area lighting and bright-day feeling.
	806 Medium Yellow	Less green than 10. Unflattering in acting areas. Useful for contrast lighting, accents, and hot-day sunlight.
	807 Dark Lemon	Darker than 806 with a higher red content.

Supergel	*Roscolene*	*Applications*
	813 Light Amber	Dark pink amber. Sunlight. Deep sunsets.
19 Fire		Strong red amber. Excellent for fire effects.
	815 Golden Amber	Useful for torchlight and light from wood fires. Use with great care. Destroys most pigment color values.
	817 Dark Amber	Useful as amber cyc light and late sunsets.
22 Deep Amber		Very useful as a backlight. Dramatic specials.
24 Scarlet		Very deep amber. Red with a touch of blue.
	819 Orange Amber	Provides excellent effect in par fixtures.
25 Orange Red	818 Orange	Same as 819. Less red.
26 Light Red		Vibrant red. Good alternate primary.
	821 Light Red	Bright red. Alternative to primary red when higher light transmission is needed.
27 Medium Red	823 Medium Red	Cycs. Good red primary for use with three-color light primary systems in cyc lighting, footlights, and border lights.
45 Rose	832 Rose Pink	Use on scenery and background effects. Adds tone and modeling to scenery.
46 Magenta	837 Medium Magenta	Uses similar to those of 45 when more saturation is needed.
48 Rose Purple		Pale evening color. Excellent for backlight.
	838 Dark Magenta	Greater intensity than 48.
	839 Rose Purple	Greater intensity than 838.
49 Medium Purple		Darkest of the magenta purple range.

Supergel	*Roscolene*	*Applications*
	843 Medium Lavender	Excellent for nighttime scenes. Rich, vivid accents. Good in backgrounds. Unrealistic.
	846 Medium Purple	Midnight and moonlight illusions. Enforces mysterious mood. Useful for evening cyc wash.
76 Light Green Blue	858 Light Green Blue	Distinctive greenish blues. Useful for romantic moonlight.
	859 Green Blue	Moonlight.
	860 Bright Blue (greener)	
	862 True Blue (bluer)	
79 Bright Blue		Cool, clear, bright blue.
	857 Medium Blue	Primary blue. For use with three-color light primary system in eye lighting.
	861 Surprise Blue	
	863 Dark Medium Blue (greener)	Good for nonrealistic night skies.
	866 Dark Urban Blue	Extremely dark blue. Highly saturated. Useful for crossover lights.
86A Pea Green	878 Yellow Green	Good for dense foliage and woodland effects.
89 Moss Green	871 Light Green	Useful for mood, mystery, and toning.
90 Dark Yellow Green	874 Medium Green	Alternative primary when higher transmission is desired.
94 Kelly Green		Fantasy and unrealistic effects. Unflattering on skin tones.

Supergel		*Roscolene*		*Applications*
95	Medium Blue Green	877	Medium Blue Green	Used on foliage in moonlight areas or for creating a mood of mystery. Good for toning scenery painted in blues, blue-greens, and greens.
		880	Light Gray	Usually used in combination with light tints of color. Reduces the brightness of color but does not affect hue or saturation. Useful when dimmer control or lower wattage lamp is not practical.
		882	Light Chocolate	Warms light and reduces intensity.
100	Frost	801	Frost	
101	Light Frost	883	Medium Gray	
104	Tough Silk			
113	Matte Silk			
114	Hamburg Frost			
120	Red Diffusion			
121	Blue Diffusion			
122	Green Diffusion			
123	Amber Diffusion			

Compiled by Thom Daly, Mitchell Gottlieb, and Jon C. Oleinick, Rosco Laboratories, Port Chester, NY 10573.

CIRCUIT LAWS
AND CABLE WIRING

OHM'S LAW

The relation between voltage, current, and resistance in a circuit is defined by Ohm's law, which is simply stated by the following formula:

$$E = IR$$

where E is in volts, I is in amperes, and R is in ohms. This can also be stated as follows:

$$I = E/R$$

or

$$R = E/I$$

RESISTORS IN SERIES

To find the total resistance in a series circuit, simply add together all resistors. In other words, a 10-ohm, a 150-ohm, and a 1,000-ohm resistor connected in series would equal a single 1,160-ohm resistor. The formula is shown in Figure B–1.

$$R_T = R_1 + R_2 + R_3 + R_4 + \text{ ---}$$

Figure B–1. Formula to define resistance in a series circuit.

RESISTORS IN PARALLEL

Resistors in a parallel circuit are a little more difficult. The formula for two resistors in parallel is as follows:

$$\text{Total resistance} = \frac{R1 \times R2}{R1 + R2}$$

For more than two resistors in parallel, the formula is given in Figure B–2.

CAPACITORS IN SERIES

Capacitors in series are similar to resistors in parallel in that one adds the reciprocals. The formula for two capacitors in series is as follows:

$$\text{Total capacitance} = \frac{C1 \times C2}{C1 + C2}$$

The formula for more than two capacitors in series is shown in Figure B–3.

$$R_T = \frac{1}{\dfrac{1}{R_1} + \dfrac{1}{R_2} + \dfrac{1}{R_3} +}$$

Figure B–2. Formula to define total resistance.

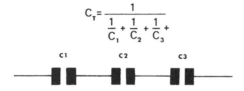

Figure B–3. Formula for more than two capacitors in series.

CAPACITORS IN PARALLEL

Capacitors behave in direct contrast to resistors. When capacitors are in parallel, use the formula shown in Figure B–4.

POWER IN A CIRCUIT

When current passes through a component, energy is given off in the form of heat. Resistors normally are associated with this action because it is part of their purpose. When it is necessary to know how much power a resistor is giving off, use the following formula:

$$W = EI$$

where W is in watts, E is in volts, and I is in amperes.

CABLE WIRING

There is no common standard of wiring for concert equipment. It is important to check the wiring standard and color coding of any connecting cables being used, whether they carry signal level, speaker level, or power (Figure B–5).

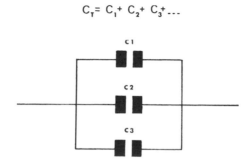

Figure B–4. Formula for capacitors in parallel.

An incorrectly wired cable can destroy the performance of an entire sound or lighting system. A faulty cable is potentially dangerous; take special care when handling main power cables and connectors. Most consoles have phase-reverse switches so that they can accommodate any standard of wiring for inputs. Phasing must be consistent throughout the system so that no phase cancellation occurs. The wiring standards for all equipment in use must be established and a record kept with the equipment for reference.

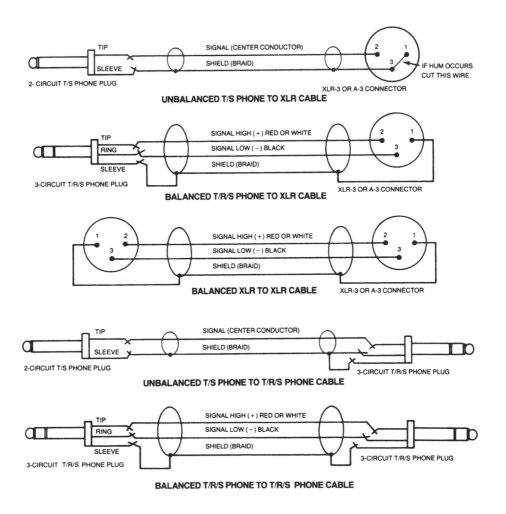

Figure B–5.   Audio cable connector wiring. Standard wiring method for audio signal cables. (Courtesy Yamaha Music.)

PRODUCTION CHECKLISTS

Production checklists help avoid any problems associated with presenting a show. With the checklist, one can identify most problems and arrange for suitable alternatives before the show. Always call ahead and check each detail to ensure a coordinated and smooth procedure. The following is a hypothetical checklist for a tour with an indoor performance requiring two semitrailers and nine touring crew members. Each show has different requirements.

Day:	Wednesday
Date:	10-6-88
City:	Anytown
Venue:	Apollo
Address:	879 Desert Hwy
Phone number:	418-267-3521

Show Times

Sound check:	4:30 PM
Doors open:	7:00 PM
Opening act:	8:00 PM
Changeover:	8:40 PM
Showtime:	9:10 PM

Call Times

Rigging:	8:00 AM
Lighting:	9:00 AM
Sound:	10:00 AM
Set:	11:00 AM
Band equipment:	Noon

Contacts

Venue technical manager:	Bert Smith
Promoter's representative:	Harry Jones
Opening act contact:	Steve Normal
Security:	Peter Muscle
Catering:	Sharon Lunch

Venue Description

Capacity:	4,720
Shape:	proscenium hall
Construction material:	concrete and steel
Age of building:	18 years
Highest seat:	32 feet above stage
Fire law restrictions:	control cables must be placed in duct
Proscenium width:	54 feet
Air conditioning:	exhaust system
Pyrotechnics restrictions:	fire marshal must be in attendance

Load In

Access:	loading dock rear of stage
Clearance:	9 feet 6 inches
Distance to stage:	25 feet
Difficulties:	none
Loading lights:	yes

Parking

Trucks:	2 trucks on dock
Cars:	20 spaces

Buses:	near loading dock
Limousines:	at stage door

Forklifts

Height capacity:	15 feet
Weight capacity:	2,000 pounds
Fuel:	propane
Tires:	pneumatic

Stage

Size available:	fixed; 60 feet wide, 54 feet deep
Size of modules:	N/A
Type:	wood
Stairs:	N/A; level with dock and dressing rooms
Masking:	black front

Soundwings

Size available:	16 feet wide, 8 feet deep
Type:	side of stage

Barricade

Type:	fixed
Height:	4 feet
Distance from stage:	4 feet
Width:	full width of stage

Mixing Positions

Sound console:	house center
Lighting console:	house center
Other:	N/A
Cable route to console:	through duct

Power

Service 1:	600 A, three phase	Distance to stage:	on stage left
Service 2:	200 A, three phase	Distance to stage:	on stage left
Service 3:	100 A, three phase	Distance to stage:	on stage right

Rigging

Beam to floor:	47 feet
Beam to ceiling:	6 feet
Beam to beam, up and downstage:	12 feet
Beam to beam, cross stage:	8 feet (no central beam)
Weight limits:	20,000 pounds
Catwalks:	adjacent to beams

Spotlights

Number available:	four
Type:	xenon troupers
Intercom:	not suitable

Houselight Control

Type:	quartz
Control location:	stage left
Dimmable:	yes

Catering

Facilities available:	kitchen and dining room
Meal times:	breakfast 7:30 AM
	lunch 1:00 PM
	dinner 6:00 PM

Dressing Rooms

Performers:	two very large rooms with bathrooms
Opening act:	1 large room, no bathroom
Tuning room:	adjacent to stage
Production office with telephone:	yes; off stage left

Other Facilities Available

Laundry:	no
Photocopier:	yes; in booking office
Work lights:	yes
Drapes for acoustic treatment:	N/A
Drapes for masking:	yes

Ladders: 16 foot A frame, Tallescope

Video: no

Local Staff Required

STAGE HANDS

Minimum call: 3 hours

Breaks required: after 4 hours

Call times and numbers: 8:00 AM, 8 hands

LOADERS

Minimum call: 3 hours

Call times and numbers: 8:00 AM, 4 loaders

Breaks required: after 4 hours

FOLLOW SPOT OPERATORS

Minimum call: 3 hours

Call times and numbers: 7:30 PM, 4 operators

PIANO TUNER

Time required: 2:00 PM

Piano type: electrical/acoustical CP70

ELECTRICIAN

Time required to connect: 8:00 AM

Time required to disconnect: 11:00 PM

RIGGERS

Time required: 8:00 AM

Climbing: two

Ground work: one

FORKLIFT DRIVER

Time required: N/A

RUNNER

Time required: 8:00 AM with vehicle

OVERNIGHT SECURITY

Time required: N/A

Number of guards: N/A

Additional Outdoor Checklist

Generators

Power capacity

Generator fuel

Scaffolding

Mixing tower

Roof

Tarpaulins

Plastic

Raincoats

Work lights

Power feed cable

Access to mix tower

Budget Items

Stage

Sound wings

Mixing platform

Barrier

Roof

Sound system

Lighting system

Equipment transport

Personnel transport

Follow spots

Follow spot operators

Stagehands

Loaders

Riggers

Forklifts

Forklift driver

Piano tuner

Electrician

Runner

Telephones

Risers

Weatherproofing

Fuel

Drapes for masking

Drapes for acoustic treatment

Dressing rooms

Generators

Generator fuel

Accommodations

Catering

Security

Crew

SAFETY AWARENESS

Workers in the live music industry are exposed to hazards and risks. To ensure safety and reduce risk to the vanishing point, a safety assessment has to be conducted as a matter of routine before any task is begun. Most safety regulations entail reasonable and practical precautions. Your safety and that of your artists and the paying public have to be considered all the time. Safety ultimately is a matter of using caution with common sense. Learn first aid.

ELECTRICAL SAFETY

Always meter the supply before connection.

Always isolate the supply before connection. Never replace a fuse with one of greater value. Never disconnect grounds.

Lay any excess cable in a figure of eight, never coiled in a circle.

RIGGING SAFETY

Never stand under a moving load.

Wear a harness when working at heights.

Learn how to tie knots efficiently.

Never stand directly under riggers working overhead.

Never use frayed or damaged slings.

Always double check all rigging procedures.

Always secure tools to your harness when working at heights.

FIRE SAFETY

Never block fire exits or fire equipment.

Always check smoke detectors before using smoke machines.

Know the position of the nearest electrical extinguishers.

SOUND LEVEL SAFETY

Prolonged exposure to high sound levels can cause hearing loss. The recommended maximum audience exposure in the United Kingdom is 104 dBA (not regulated in the United States) over the duration of the event. Wear hearing protection when exposed to high levels for long periods.

PUBLIC SAFETY

Never leave electrical connections in public areas unsupervised.

Never expose an audience to any danger.

Make sure that equipment is kept secure from the public.

FURTHER READING

Ballou, Glen M. *Handbook for Sound Engineers: The New Audio Cyclopedia,* 2d ed. New York: Macmillan, 1991.

Baskerville, David. *Music Business Handbook and Career Guide,* 5th ed. Peru, IL: Sherwood, 1990.

Borwick, John. *Loudspeaker and Headphone Handbook.* Boston: Butterworth–Heinemann, 1988.

Capel, Vivian. *Public Address Systems.* Boston: Butterworth–Heinemann, 1992.

Davis, Don, and Carolyn Davis. *Sound System Engineering,* 2d ed. Englewood Cliffs, NJ: Sams, 1987.

Davis, Gary, and Ralph Jones. *The Sound Reinforcement Handbook,* 2d ed. Milwaukee, WI: Hal Leonard, 1988.

Eargle, John. *Handbook of Sound System Design.* Elar, 1989.

Giddings, Philip. *Audio Systems Design and Installation.* New York: Macmillan, 1990.

Harris, Cyril M. *Handbook of Acoustical Measurements and Noise Control.* New York: McGraw-Hill, 1991.

Huntington, John. *Control Systems for Live Entertainment.* Boston: Focal Press, 1994.

Moody, James L. *Concert Lighting: Techniques: Art and Business.* Boston: Focal Press, 1989.

Strong, William J., and George R. Plitnick. *Music Speech Audio*. Norwalk, CT: Soundprints, 1992.

Thompson, George, ed. *The Focal Guide to Safety in Live Performance*. Boston: Focal Press, 1993.

Trubitt, David, ed. *Concert Sound*. Milwaukee, WI: Hal Leonard, 1993.

GLOSSARY

absorption   Damping of a sound wave passing through a medium or striking a surface. The property of materials, objects, or media to absorb sound energy.

AC   Abbreviation for *alternating current*, which is an electric current that keeps reversing its direction.

acoustics   The science of sound. The factors that determine the quality of received sound in a room or auditorium.

ad lib   To cover an unexpected situation in a show or hide a lapse of memory.

alignment   The process of setting controls and functions for optimum system performance.

ambience   The combination of reverberation and background noise that characterizes the sound of a given room.

ampere   The common unit of current; the rate of flow of electricity; abbreviated A.

amplifier   An electronic device for magnifying electrical signals to a level to which speakers respond.

amplitude   The peak of a sound waveform.

analog   Electronic signal the waveform of which resembles that of the original signal, as opposed to digital.

anechoic   Without echo. In an anechoic chamber the walls are lined with a material that completely absorbs any sound.

arc light   A lamp with a carbon-arc discharge as the source of illumination.

arena   A venue where the audience is seated to the sides of the stage as well as the front.

attack time   The time taken for the onset of gain reduction in a compressor.

attenuation   The reduction of level at the source.

auto transformer   An iron-cored coil across an AC supply that allows various voltages to be selected.

azimuth   The angle between the gap of a tape head and the tape.

baffle   General term for a wall, board, or enclosure that carries a speaker. The baffle separates the front and back radiations from the speaker; they would otherwise cancel each other out.

balanced line   Program cable in which twin signal wires are isolated from the earth.

bandwidth   The interval between cutoff frequencies.

barndoors   A metal fitting attached to the front of a flood light that allows the light to be cut off by two or four hinged flaps.

base   The part of a lamp to which the electrical connection is made. Also the mechanical support of the lamp.

bass   Low-frequency end of the audio spectrum.

bass reflex   Type of speaker cabinet with an outlet (port) that allows enclosed air to improve the efficiency at low frequencies. This is caused by inversion of phase within the enclosure so that the radiations from the port aid the radiations from the cone.

batten   A length of rigid material hung on spot lines in a theater.

beam   The cone of light from a lighting instrument.

beam light   A light with no lens that gives a parallel beam.

black light   Ultraviolet light.

boom   Vertical pipe for hanging lamps. An extendable arm on a microphone stand for supporting microphones.

border   An abbreviated drop. Used for masking trusses and fly bars.

break jack   A jack arranged to break the normal circuit when a plug is inserted.

bridle   The wire ropes that attach to chain motors to achieve the correct rigging position with available rigging points.

bulb   The glass or quartz part of a lamp that encloses the filament or electrodes.

bus bar   Common earth or other contact wire.

cans   Term for headphones.

carbon arc   Light produced by gaseous discharge between two cerium-cored carbon rods. These rods burn for a limited time; an operator must maintain the intensity and sharpness of the light.

cardioid microphone   A microphone with a heart-shaped directivity pattern.

channel   Sequence of circuits or components handling one specific signal.

circuit breaker   A device used instead of a fuse to open a circuit automatically when it is overloaded.

clamp   Devices used to attach lamps to pipes or trusses. C and G clamps are so called because of their shapes.

clipping   Distortion in a mixer or amplifier caused by severe overloading.

compression   The process of reducing dynamic range. A compressed signal has a higher dynamic range.

compressor   A variable-gain amplifier in which the gain is controlled by the input signal; used to reduce dynamic range.

concert pitch   System of tuning music based on a frequency of A = 440 Hz.

condenser microphone   Type of microphone in which the signal is generated by the variation of capacitance between the diaphragm and a fixed plate.

counterweight system   A mechanical system for flying lamps, drapes, and scenery with a counterweight that runs up and down a track at the side of the stage.

cross fade   To fade in one channel while fading out another.

crossover   A unit for dividing a signal into separate frequency bands.

crossover frequency   The transition frequency at which the crossover splits the signal.

crosstalk   Unwanted breakthrough from adjacent channels.

cue   A point at which certain adjustments are required during a performance.

cue sheet   A record of the scenes and changes for each segment of the show.

curtain   A drape that hides the stage from the audience.

cyc light   A light fitting with a specially shaped reflector that produces a broad, elongated light beam; enables a cyclorama to be lit evenly overall from a relatively close distance.

cyclorama   A stretch of taut vertical cloth used as a general-purpose scenic background. Also called *cyc*.

damping   Process of reducing unwanted resonant effects by applying absorbent material to a speaker cabinet. Poor damping allows the motion of the speaker to continue once the signal has been removed, creating a booming sound that masks clarity.

DC   Abbreviation for *direct current*. Current that flows in one direction only, unlike AC.

decay time   The recovery time of a compressor or other processing device for the circuit to return to normal once the signal has been removed.

decibel   The smallest change in loudness detected by the average human ear; abbreviated dB. Zero decibels is the threshold of human hearing. The threshold of pain is between 120 and 130 dB. The decibel is a ratio, not an absolute number, and is used to identify the relation between true power, voltage, and sound pressure levels. Decibels alone have no specific meaning. For example, dBV is a voltage ratio; 0 dB = 0.775 V root mean square (RMS). Decibels SPL is the sound pressure level ratio. It is used to measure acoustic pressure. Decibels BM is a power ratio. Decibels A takes into account the unequal sensitivity of the ear, and sound pressure level is measured through a circuit that compensates for this equal loudness. These measurements are termed *A weighted*.

diffraction   The manner in which sound can bend around obstacles.

diffuser   Translucent material used in front of lamps to soften and disperse the light quality and reduce intensity.

digital sound   The process of converting a normal analog signal into a series of numerical measurements that can be transmitted as digital code.

dimmer   An electrical circuit that regulates the current flowing through the lamps to which it is connected, thus allowing adjustment of lighting intensity.

direct injection   The process of feeding an electronic musical instrument directly to the control console rather than through a microphone.

dispersion   The extent to which light rays or sound waves are scattered or diffused.

downstage   The position at front of the stage closest to the audience.

drop   A cloth suspended from fly bars or a grid to mask the stage; a backdrop.

dynamic range   The range of signal levels from lowest to highest. A program with wide dynamic range has a large variation between the loudest and quietest parts.

echo   Sound that has been reflected and arrives with such a magnitude and time interval after the direct sound as to be a distinguishable repeat of the original.

ellipsoidal spotlight   A spotlight in which the light collected from an ellipsoidal reflector (mirror) is focused on a lens. The shape of the light beam is adjustable with an internal variable iris, silhouette stencil (gobo), or independent framing shutters. Most of these lamps are designed to project perforated metal gobos.

EPROM   Erasable programmable read-only memory.

expander   An amplifier that increases gain as the input level increases; a characteristic that stretches dynamic range.

feedback   Signal from the output of system that returns to the input, creating unwanted oscillation that can quickly become out of control and cause severe damage to speaker components.

flash through   A check of the lighting system one channel at a time.

flat   A unit section of scenery; a tall screen.

flies   The space above the stage occupied by sets of lines, hanging drapes, and lamps.

flood   A type of light fitting that illuminates a wide area.

fluorescent lamp   A tubular lamp in which a mercury vapor discharge energizes a fluorescent powder coating on the inside of the tube.

fly   To lift equipment above the stage with electrical chain hoists or on a counterweight system.

focus   To position lamps so that the beams light the desired areas.

FOH   Front of house; the front of an auditorium, the end opposite the stage.

foldback   The term given to signals returning from the house console to the stage. Foldback becomes a monitoring system when a separate console is used to control the on-stage monitors.

follow spot   High-intensity lamp that requires an operator to follow the subject being lit and to control intensity and color.

frammel   A strip of wood placed between speaker cabinets to separate and angle them vertically to reduce phase interference between cabinets.

frequency   The rate of repetition of signal, measured in hertz (Hz).

Fresnel lens   A lens with a surface composed of a series of concentric ribs of stepped cross sections, making it thinner, lighter, and more efficient than a solid lens.

fuse   Protective device for an electrical circuit to prevent overloading.

gaffer tape   A wide, plasticized cloth tape with many uses in concert production.

gain   The increase in signal power from one point to another.

gel   Color filter. Originally made of gelatin, color filters are now made of plastic.

gobo   A metal stencil placed in the gate of a profile spot to shape the beam of light.

graphic equalizer   An equalizer that has slider-level controls; once set, the sliders represent the response curve.

grid   The framework of trusses from which lamps are hung.

ground row   Series of lamps in the form of troughs laid on the ground to illuminate a cyclorama or other background.

harmonic distortion   A form of distortion in which unwanted harmonics are added to the original signal.

harmonics   Overtones that are multiples of the fundamental tone that shape the waveform and make it possible to differentiate instruments even when they are playing the same note.

headroom   The space, usually expressed in decibels (dB), between the operating level and the maximum available level. Inadequate headroom distorts transient peaks.

hertz   The unit of frequency. One hertz equals one cycle per second; abbreviated Hz.

hiss   Noise that sounds like prolonged sibilant sounds.

house lights   Auditorium lighting.

hue   The predominant sensation of color.

hum   Electrical interference caused at main frequency, 50/60 Hz.

impedance   The degree to which a circuit impedes the flow of alternating current. Measured in ohms.

induction   Production of current across a space caused by electrical or magnetic fields.

infinite baffle   Speaker mounting that allows no air paths between front and rear of speaker.

instrument   General name for lighting fixtures.

intensity   Of light, the power of a light source, its brightness. Of sound, the objective strength of sound, loudness.

inverse square law   An equation relating the intensity of light to the distance from an object.

iris   An adjustable circular shutter used in a profile spot to vary the size of the beam.

jack   Terminating point of a circuit. Common term for phone plug connector.

lamp   General term for an incandescent light source (bulb, bubble). Also used as a general term for any lighting instrument.

LED   Light-emitting diode.

leg   A narrow strip of drape used to mask the sides of the stage.

Leko   A brand of ellipsoidal profile spot.

lighting plot   A scale plan diagram indicating the positions and types of lamps used. Details of color, cabling, accessories, patching, and trim height may be included.

limiter   A type of compressor that fixes a ceiling of maximum level without changing the dynamic range below the threshold.

line level   Preamplified signal, in contrast to microphone level. Actual signal levels vary; nominal microphone level is –50 dBM, and nominal line level is +4 dBM.

loudness   The subjective impression of the strength of sound.

luminaire   A complete lighting unit; consists of a lamp with parts designed to distribute light, position and protect the lamp, and connect the lamp to the power supply.

luminary   A light source.

mask   To conceal equipment from an audience.

matrix   Electronics for accepting several signals and giving one output.

microphone   A transducer for converting acoustic energy to electrical energy.

MIDI   Musical instrument digital interface.

mirror ball   A spherical ball with a surface covered in small plane mirrors. Multiple moving spots of light shine from the ball when it is lit and rotated.

mixer   The electronics that allow the combination of several signals in desired proportions.

modulation   The control of one waveform by another.

monitor   A speaker cabinet fed with signal to provide information needed by a performer.

multiplexer   Unit for encoding and decoding multiplex signals.

noise   Any unwanted sound.

noise gate   An amplifier that has zero output until the input level exceeds a chosen threshold level.

nook light   Small, open-fronted trough fitting with a short strip light and curved reflector.

notch filter   An equalizer with a very narrow bandwidth.

octave   The interval between a given tone and its repetition eight tones above or below on the musical scale. A note an octave higher than another note is twice the frequency of the first note.

off stage   A position outside the performing area.

omnidirectional microphone   A microphone that is equally sensitive in all directions.

on stage   In the performing area.

open circuit   A circuit that is not continuous and cannot pass current.

oscillator   A device for producing continuous oscillation or a pure tone at any desired frequency.

oscilloscope   A device for visual display of electronic waveforms.

PA   Abbreviation for public address system; alternative term for sound system.

pad   A series of resistors to introduce a fixed amount of gain reduction for impedance-matching purposes.

pan   In lighting, to move the beam of a lamp from side to side of the stage. In sound, to alter the position of a signal laterally.

par light   A tungsten-halogen (quartz) lamp in which a parabolic aluminized reflector forms part of the bulb. The internally silvered reflector, together with the molded lens front glass, provide a fixed beam. Par bulbs are available in various beam sizes.

parametric equalizer   An equalizer that can vary frequency, level, and bandwidth.

patching   The term used for connecting cables in the correct circuits.

phantom power   Method of sending DC supply to a condenser microphone or direct box by means of connecting the positive side to both signal wires of a balanced line and the negative to the screen.

phase   The position that a waveform has reached at any given instant in the cycle. Waves are in phase when their cycle positions coincide.

pink noise   Pink noise is white noise that has passed through a filter to bring the response to an equal energy level (per octave) as heard by the human ear.

pitch   Subjective effect of sound related mainly to frequency but also affected by intensity and harmonic structure.

potentiometer   A variable resistor used for volume and tone controls. Commonly called a *pot*.

prefade listen   Facility available on mixing consoles for listening to a signal before it is fed to the main program outputs.

presence   Quality of immediacy. Boosting the upper middle frequencies achieves presence.

profile spot   A lamp with a beam that can be either soft or hard.

proscenium   The wall dividing the stage from the auditorium. The opening through which the audience views the stage is called the proscenium opening.

pyrotechnics   Any bangs, flashes, or explosions.

RAM   Random access memory. Memory (information) that can be written in or read out in any order.

recovery time   The time taken for a compressor or limiter to restore the gain to normal when the signal is reduced.

resonance   The tendency of any physical body to vibrate most freely at a particular frequency because of excitation by a sound with that particular frequency.

reverberation   The sustaining effect of multiple sound reflections in an enclosed area.

ribbon microphone   Microphone that operates with a thin metal ribbon suspended in a magnetic field.

rig   To install and set up equipment in required position. The finished assembly of lamps positioned, patched, and focused for a performance.

rostrum   A scenic platform, a riser.

rumble   Low-frequency vibration.

scrim   Thin netting (gauze) used to provide translucent eyes or create scenic diffusion.

set   A group of risers arranged to give a decorative effect.

sightlines   Theoretical lines indicating what the audience can see.

signal to noise ratio   The ratio of the desired signal to residual system noise.

silhouette   A pictorial style that concentrates on subject outline for its effect. Surface detail, tone, texture, and color are suppressed.

silicon chip   A method of fabricating resistors and transistors into miniaturized circuits on a wafer of silicon, which is cased in a plastic or ceramic body with leads bonded onto the silicon.

spanset   An endless loop of nylon strands used for rigging purposes. Because the spanset is a soft sling, it can be used for a variety of rigging applications. Spansets are color coded for weight loading.

special   A light performing a particular function.

spiking   Marking a position on the stage.

strike   To remove a piece of set or equipment from the performing area.

tab   Any curtain.

talkback   Headphone intercom system.

teaser   A border used to mask trusses or fly bars.

threshold   The point above which level changes take place.

throw   The distance from the light to the object being lit.

tilt   The vertical movement of a light.

transformer   Component with two coils of wire, the primary and secondary, the lengths of which are in a fixed ratio to allow voltages to be increased or decreased and circuit impedances to be matched for maximum power transfer.

translucent   Allowing light to pass through without being transparent.

tree   A high stand or tower with horizontal arms for mounting lamps.

trim   For the grid, to level a grid or truss. For the dimmers, to adjust dimmer response to control voltage. Dimmers out of trim do not give the subtle control needed for stage lighting.

unidirectional microphone   A microphone sensitive to sound from one direction only.

upstage   The stage area toward the back, away from the audience.

UHF   Ultra high frequency (about 30 to 1,000 MHz).

VCA   Voltage-controlled amplifier, used instead of faders to control channel gain in a sound control console.

VHF   Very high frequency (about 30 to 300 MHz).

volt   The unit of electrical force.

VU meter   A meter for indicating program volume that gives signal power, in decibels, on a steady tone and volume units (percentage utilization of the channel) on program.

wavelength   The distance between corresponding parts of a waveform.

white noise   A full audio spectrum signal with the same energy level at all frequencies.

windshield (popshield)   A foam sock placed over a microphone to reduce the amount of wind amplified.

wings   The areas on either side of the stage.

zero level   The level used for lining up audio equipment. Zero decibels equals 1 mW. This corresponds to 0.775 V root means square (RMS) across a resistance of 600 ohms.

zoom lens   A variable-focus lens.

INDEX

Page numbers followed by "f" denote figures.